Plant-Based Diet After 50

The Complete Guide to Vegan Diet with 21-Day Meal Plan Designed Specifically for Men and Women Over 50, Including Healthy and Delicious Recipes

ANNE MERRITT

Copyright © 2020 Anne Merritt
All rights reserved.

No part of this publication may be reproduced, distributed, or transmitted in any form or by any means, including photocopying, recording, or other electronic or mechanical methods, except as permitted by U.S. copyright law.

Legal Notice:

This book is copyright protected. This book is only for personal use. You cannot amend, distribute, sell, use, quote or paraphrase any part, or the content within this book, without the consent of the author or publisher.

Disclaimer Notice:

Please note the information contained within this document is for educational and entertainment purposes only. All effort has been executed to present accurate, up to date, and reliable, complete information. No warranties of any kind are declared or implied. Readers acknowledge that the author is not engaging in the rendering of legal, financial, medical or professional advice. The content within this book has been derived from various sources. Please consult a licensed professional before attempting any techniques outlined in this book.

Although the author and publisher have made every effort to ensure that the information in this book was correct at press time, the author and publisher do not assume and hereby disclaim any liability to any party for any loss, damage, or disruption caused by errors or omissions, whether such errors or omissions result from negligence, accident, or any other cause.

CONTENTS

INTRODUCTION 1

CHAPTER 1: CONNECTIONS BETWEEN A PLANT-BASED DIET AND AGING 2

CHAPTER 2: HOW CAN A PLANT-BASED DIET PROVIDE BENEFITS FOR PEOPLE OVER 50? 5

CHAPTER 3: ENVIRONMENTAL BENEFITS OF A PLANT-BASED DIET 8

CHAPTER 4: HOW TO TRANSITION TO A PLANT-BASED DIET 12

CHAPTER 5: HOW TO EAT FOR HEALTHY AGING ON A PLANT-BASED DIET 18

CHAPTER 6: PLANT-BASED DIET AND WEIGHT LOSS 20

CHAPTER 7: OTHER HEALTHY HABITS 25

21-DAY MEAL PLAN 30

BREAKFAST RECIPES 36

    Grapes and Green Tea Smoothie 36

    Mango and Kale Smoothie 37

    Pomegranate Smoothie 37

    Coconut Water Smoothie 38

    Apple, Banana, and Berry Smoothie 39

    Berry Ginger Zing Smoothie 39

    Dragon Fruit Smoothie Bowl 40

    Chocolate Smoothie Bowl 41

    Zucchini and Blueberry Smoothie 42

    Hot Pink Beet Smoothie 43

    Chickpea Flour Frittata 43

    Potato Pancakes 45

Chocolate Chip Pancakes 46

Turmeric Steel-Cut Oats 47

Vegetable Pancakes 48

Banana and Chia Pudding 49

Tofu Scramble 50

Pumpkin Spice Oatmeal 52

Peanut Butter Bites 52

Maple and Cinnamon Overnight Oats 53

Beans on Toast 54

LUNCH RECIPES 56

Brussels Sprout Skewers 56

Thai Peanut Butter Cauliflower Wings 57

Potato Salad 58

Carrot Patties 59

Eggplant and Potatoes in Tomato Sauce 60

Grilled Mushrooms with Garlic Sauce 61

Sesame Tofu and Veggies Noodles 62

Bombay Potatoes and Peas 64

BBQ Tofu Pizza 66

Quinoa Tacos 67

Teriyaki Noodle Stir-Fry 69

Garlicky Tofu 70

Mac and Cheese 71

Peanut Butter and Pumpkin Soup 72

Sweet Korean Lentils 73

Pasta Puttanesca 74

Walnut Meat Tacos 75

Couscous with Olives 76

- Black Bean and Corn Salad 78
- Chickpea Salad Sandwich 79
- Ginger Veggie Stir-Fry 80

DINNER RECIPES 81
- Mushroom Sliders 81
- Lentil and Turnip Soup 82
- Tomato and Chickpea Curry 83
- Lentil Stroganoff 84
- Broccoli and Sun-dried Tomato Pasta 85
- Creamy Broccoli Pasta 86
- Wild Rice Mushroom Soup 87
- Kung Pao Lentils 89
- Orange Tofu 90
- Lentil Brown Rice Soup 92
- Peanut and Lentil Soup 93
- Lentil with Spinach 95
- Lentil and Quinoa Loaf 96
- Chorizo 98
- Spiced Carrot and Millet Salad 99
- Carrots and Quinoa Veggie Bowl 100
- Pasta Primavera 101
- Chickpea Burgers 102
- Wild Rice Soup 104
- Sesame Cauliflower 105
- Potato Curry 106

DESSERT RECIPES 108
- Raspberry Muffins 108
- Chocolate Chip Cake 109

- Coffee Cake 110
- Chocolate Marble Cake 112
- Chocolate Chip Cookies 113
- Lemon Cake 114
- Banana Muffins 116
- No-Bake Cookies 117
- Peanut Butter and Oat Bars 118
- Baked Apples 119
- Chocolate Strawberry Shake 120
- Chocolate Clusters 120
- Banana Coconut Cookies 121
- Chocolate Pots 122
- Maple and Tahini Fudge 123
- Creamsicles 123
- Peanut Butter, Nut, and Fruit Cookies 124
- Chocolate Covered Dates 125
- Hot Chocolate 126
- Vanilla Cupcakes 127
- Chocolate Mug Cake 128

CONCLUSION 129

ABOUT THE AUTHOR 130

INTRODUCTION

The global population of adults over 60 years is expected to double by 2050, from 840 million to 2 billion. This is a staggering number and poses a huge problem for any country's healthcare system. This isn't just a problem for healthcare professionals. This is our everyday problem right now.

On a smaller scale, aging brings about many problems. Aside from aesthetic deterioration, the aging population is now faced with a plethora of diseases that make life difficult for them. Some are chronic diseases that can haunt you for the rest of your life, partially because of the pain it brings and the steep treatment cost depending on where you live.

That said, things do not have to be this way. There are a few ways you can combat aging. One of them is through a change in diet. In this book, we will talk about plant-based diets and everything you need to know to get started.

Keep in mind that this is not a miracle cure, nor will it give quick results. However, what is certain is that this is a long-term investment that will be well worth it in the long run. By going green, you are doing more than just nourishing your body and restoring your youth. You are also helping a movement to reverse the damage done to the planet and other animals. To some people, going vegan is more than just a lifestyle change. It is a campaign to save the planet.

But perhaps you are not interested in that sentiment and just want to lose weight. Regardless of what your end-goal is, be it losing weight, combat aging, or saving the planet, going vegan is one way to do it. Ready to get started? Read on!

CHAPTER 1: CONNECTIONS BETWEEN A PLANT-BASED DIET AND AGING

It's already been well-established that eating lots of veggies is good for your health. The real question now is, how is it good for your health? Some diets, such as vegan diets, take it to the next step by restricting you to plant-based meals. What good will it do for your body? Plenty.

You see, regardless of your age, anti-aging is always a concern for many people after the age of 25. This is about the time when your body stops producing collagen. From then, aging will show, and people will go to extreme lengths to slow it down.

Of course, to say that there is a way to stop or even reverse aging altogether is false as there is no such thing. Otherwise, we would all be immortal. The whole idea behind anti-aging is to make you appear younger, but that also has its limits.

You can indeed slow the process of aging by making your muscle tone more prominent, your collagen firmer, your skin tighter, thus making you look younger than you actually are. But this comes at a cost that increases as you age. Younger people do not have to put in that much effort to look dashing, but older people may need to make a complete lifestyle overhaul to do the same. It all depends on what you eat, what exercise you do, and how much sleep you get.

Therefore, much of what you do to slow aging has to do with what you put in your body, not on your body. In other words, skincare products can only go so far. According to The American Journal of Epidemiology, the best way to combat aging is to provide your body with all the right nutrients.

A diet consisting of fruits, veggies, whole grains, and low in sodium, processed meats, and sugar can help with cellular aging. That means your cells would be healthier and your chance of developing some chronic diseases decreases. Emphasis needs to be placed on improving the quality of one's diet as a whole instead of prioritizing eating more of just one food item or nutrients.

The Lancet Oncology also published a study, stating that maybe anti-aging does not have to be that tedious. You might just need to adapt to a plant-based diet and cut down on meat and dairy in some cases. The study looked at the health and length of our cell's chromosome caps, known as Telomeres.

Telomeres protect your cell's DNA as well as promotes stability. They function as a protective cap that also helps rebuild our DNA structure. Keeping the cell's DNA intact and stable means preventing cellular breakdown, which leads to aging. They also determine how fast a cell can regenerate itself, and age is the best predictor of telomere length.

Many studies suggest that plant-based diet help with overall health, not just aging alone. For one, a plant-based diet may slow down our cell's deterioration by boosting enzyme activities and protecting Telomerase's length. This allows Telomerase to help slow down aging.

There are many reasons why telomeres shorten. Among them is diet. Adopting a plant-based diet helps support our cells. In fact, in just 3 months of following a plant-based diet, you can expect to see a massive improvement in telomerase health. Telomeres' health does more than just slow down aging. They also prevent certain chronic conditions such as heart disease, diabetes, and dementia.

In short, there are many health benefits to going green.

Now that the importance of telomeres is clear let's discuss how you can keep your telomeres healthy. Most plant-based foods contain many useful nutrients that aid in maintaining their health, such as:

- Vitamin C, E, and selenium: Antioxidants that prevent cell damage or cell death. Vitamin C is found in abundance in oranges, tomatoes, strawberries, grapefruit, kiwi, papaya, and leafy-green veggies.

- Folate/Folic acid: Protects the telomeres from shortening as well as helps the body produce new and healthy cells. Found in asparagus, beans, lentils, rice, and leafy-green veggies.
- Omega 3 fatty acids: Fights inflammation and also helps in protecting telomeres' length. Found in nuts, leafy-green veggies, vegetable oils, and flaxseed.

On the other hand, foods that cause inflammation, aging, and damaged cells are processed foods. They tend to contain saturated fat and excessive sodium. So you are already taking a big step in the right direction by eating processed foods minimally.

CHAPTER 2: HOW CAN A PLANT-BASED DIET PROVIDE BENEFITS FOR PEOPLE OVER 50?

Another study released by the Journal of the American College of Nutrition stresses the importance of a plant-based diet. The latest edition shows that a plant-based diet is directly linked to healthy aging. This means you could live a life free from brain, cardiovascular, or other chronic health problems.

It has already been well-established that going green is good for the body and mind. However, the study specifically focuses on healthy aging, which makes it interesting. In fact, you are 50% less likely to develop chronic diseases such as cancer, heart diseases, and type 2 diabetes if your diet is comprised mostly of veggies.

In addition to that, here are some of the benefits you can expect from a plant-based diet in terms of how they can improve your longevity and make life easier as you age.

Reduced Inflammation

Chronic inflammation, although not as famous as type 2 diabetes or cancer, plagues pretty much everyone. It causes stiffness, aches, and bloat after a meal. Most processed food and animal products are full of inflammatory triggers, such as endotoxins and saturated fat.

This can cause a lot of damage to our bodies and to our overall health. Inflammation may not kill a person directly, but it can be a massive pain. In fact, inflammation is linked to diabetes, dementia, stroke, heart disease, and other severe conditions. In contrast, a plant-based diet is low in saturated fat and endotoxins, which often contain a lot of anti-inflammatory fiber.

Lowered Cholesterol

A plant-based diet can help decrease your blood cholesterol by almost 35% since they contain no cholesterol and very little saturated fat.

Healthier Heart

A simple diet change can reduce your risk of heart disease by 42%, at least if you move from the Standard American Diet to a plant-based diet. As such, a plant-based diet not only helps prevent heart disease but also reverse it as well.

Diabetes Prevention or Reversal

Since a plant-based diet contains so little sugar, it can reduce the risk of developing type 2 diabetes by about 35%. Those who already have diabetes will find that going green can save their lives as this move alone can help the body regulate blood sugar level in as fast as 24 hours.

Lower Risk of Cancer

Adopting a plant-based diet seems to drastically lower your risk for a certain type of cancer, such as colon cancer. This is because there is a correlation between dairy consumption to breast, ovarian, and prostate cancer.

More Robust Immune System

By adding more fruits and veggies to your plate, you can naturally boost your immune system. A diet with 6 servings of fruits and veggies a day helps with antibody production and improves your immune response, making you more resilient to common illnesses.

Better Digestion

While we are on the topic of the immune system, do you know that your stomach protects you more from the outside world than your skin? A plant-based diet helps improve gut health and digestion, which means you won't have to deal with bloat after dinner.

Weight Loss

Going green helps in losing weight. This is common knowledge as whole plant-based foodstuffs are full of nutrients and low in calories compared to animal products such as meat and dairy. In other words, for the same amount of food it takes to make you feel full, you would be consuming fewer carbs if you consume a plant-based meal than one comprised of animal products.

Carbs are just one piece of the puzzle, though. Keep in mind that processed food is full of salt, saturated fat, and sugar, all of which contribute to weight gain. A plant-based diet either contain very little or none of those ingredients, which should keep your weight in check:

CHAPTER 3: ENVIRONMENTAL BENEFITS OF A PLANT-BASED DIET

There is enough evidence showing that going green can literally save not only your life but also others. Most problems in the world stem from one question: "How can we feed everyone?" This leads to the destruction of the local ecosystem by deforestation, global warming, the list goes on. With all the problems in the world, some people take it upon themselves to make it a better place, no matter how small that change may be.

You too can join in on this effort through an actionable and straightforward method to cut down your carbon footprint and protect the animals and planet for several generations. You see, the animal-based agriculture industry caused most of the environmental problems. It is hard enough to see how they raise those animals only to turn them into products on the shelves, let alone measure what environmental damage they've caused yearly. Actually, someone did measure it, and factory farms in the United States alone are responsible for 300 million tons of waste a year.

Thankfully, there is a way to keep your stomach full, your body healthy, and the earth green. Switching to a plant-based diet is a direct counter to many of the problems described above.

Cutting Your Carbon Footprint

Animal agriculture contributed so much to global warming through the production of greenhouse gases. According to the United Nations Food and Agriculture Organization (FAO), 14.5% of global greenhouse gas emissions come from livestock production alone. Even worse, some other organizations say that the number could be as high as 51%. The 300 million tons of waste a year from the United States also amounts up to 37% of agricultural greenhouse gas emissions. We would be in a much better situation if we can somehow bring the number down to zero in this department.

How can the number be this staggeringly high? Well, that is because of how the animal agriculture industry cut corners in manure management. In their "lagoons," or cesspits filled with animal waste, all that excrement produce a large amount of methane. Methane is a type of greenhouse gas that is much more dangerous than carbon dioxide produced from burning fossil fuels. This is because methane can trap heat better and heat up the planet up to 20 times compared to the same amount of carbon dioxide.

And it's not just methane that we have to worry about. The sheer scale of the transportation and energy industry put enough CO2 in the air. We could do away with as much methane as possible.

Conserving Water

Did you know how much of Earth's water is actually usable? Less than 5%. In fact, out of all that beautiful blue of Earth, only 3% of that is freshwater. In that 3% of fresh water, only 1.2% is drinkable, and the rest is either glaciers, ice caps, permafrost, or deep underground. Needless to say, we don't have much water to go around. How do we budget our water consumption?

Based on the Water Footprint Network report, you need 1,000 gallons to make a gallon of milk. It shouldn't take a genius to realize that a ratio of 1000:1 is highly inefficient. 87% percent of the U.S. water usage goes to agriculture. Considering that you need 100 times more water to produce just a pound of animal protein than a pound of grain protein, you can see how the water is better used elsewhere.

Saving Animal and Plant Habitats

One-third of arable land worldwide is used for animal agriculture alone. Most of that land is used to produce food to feed the pigs, cattle, and chickens that everybody loves to eat. For this reason, we are partly to blame for the success of the animal agriculture industry and the subsequent deforestation. Desertification is also common and is caused by grazing livestock, destroying the native vegetation, and accelerating soil erosion.

Both deforestation and desertification lead to the extinction of certain animal species such as orangutans, red pandas, and sloths. To keep their profit, animal agriculture industries also have lobbyists advocating on their behalf to limit the impact of animal rights in the United States. In the United States alone, livestock grazing impacts 14% of endangered animals and 33% of endangered plants.

Now, you might argue that going green also requires the use of all that land. That is a fair argument, except that the resource consumption for producing animal products is much higher than pure veggie-based foodstuffs. Keep in mind that all those animals need to be fed, and a lot of land is used just for that purpose. The ratio is similar to that of water consumption per gallon of milk. You would be able to feed many people for the same amount of food to raise a pig.

Dead Zones

Animal agriculture also contributes to water pollution as well. In fact, it is the leading cause of water pollution and various dead zones. Here is a little bit of insight into how the animal industry fertilizes their crops for animal feed.

Factory farms produce waste that is stored in massive lagoons. This waste is applied, most often untreated, to crop as fertilizers in large quantities. Of course, the soil could not absorb all the toxins in the manure. The toxins have to go somewhere, so they seep into the groundwater, which then flows to rivers and oceans, destroying the marine ecosystem.

This has happened on more than one occasion. A particularly disastrous one was in the Gulf of Mexico that is connected to the Mississippi River. The river was chock full of farm animal waste all the way from the Midwest, and it all poured out. Next was a total oxygen depletion from the manure and fertilizer that killed all marine life inside an 8,500 square foot dead zone.

Cleaner Air

Going to that yearly 300 million ton of manure from the Unites States, they also produce another gas called ammonia. This is the most potent form of nitrogen that contributes to smog, algae blooms, and fish deaths. Moreover, it is found that the air around factory farms contain an above-average concentration of endotoxins, particulate matter, sulfide, carbon dioxide, and methane. That cannot be good for our lungs or the atmosphere as a whole.

Eating for the Planet

With all being said, it is fair to say that the animal agriculture industry caused quite a lot of problems for the planet. They hold over half of the world's arable land resources, consume most of our already scarce freshwater resources, and produce a lot of greenhouse gas. All of this leads to air and water pollution, land degradation, and deforestation, which could lead to many animal species' extinction.

You would think that with all those resources, world hunger shouldn't exist. Unfortunately, it is still a problem today. In fact, 1 in 8 people is still suffering from food scarcity. The solution here is not investing more water, land, and forest into the animal agriculture industry. It is about using all of that resources more efficiently. We can literally feed everyone on the planet using the same amount of resources if we all switch to a plant-based diet and shut down the animal agriculture industry altogether or drastically limit its production.

The real war against clime is not being fought on the political stage. It is fought right in front of us, on our plates, many times a day, and across the planet. You have a choice in choosing which food to eat. The problem isn't a lack of awareness. Pretty much everyone knows about global warming. The problem is the lack of action. By choosing to go green, you are contributing to the effort to reverse the damage mankind has done to the planet. It might seem minuscule to you, but every little bit helps, and it all adds up on a larger scale.

CHAPTER 4: HOW TO TRANSITION TO A PLANT-BASED DIET

Depending on your current diet, going from it to a plant-based diet may be difficult. In this chapter, we will discuss how you can ease into this new healthy diet and improve your overall health altogether.

Change Your Mindset

The first few and yet most important steps are all about the mind. You must approach this transition with an open mind. Many people fail to commit to this diet because they always think of what they have to give up, such as delicious burgers or fries. Instead, maintain a positive mindset.

Think of what you would gain from this. A lot of people think that this is all about deprivation, struggle, and requiring strong willpower. That is not how you should approach any life changes. Instead, think of all the good things that will come your way after making that transition. In fact, you don't have to give up on pizzas, sandwiches, or chocolates as there are many healthy vegan alternatives out there.

In short, if you are feeling uncomfortable or bad about this whole thing, then there is a flaw in your approach. This should be something that is fun and fulfilling for you. Speaking of fulfilling…

Know the Why

When you know the "why," the "how" tends to get done. Before you embark on the plant-based journey, be clear about your goal. Why would you embark on this journey in the first place? This is a critical question to get out of the way, especially if this will be a major lifestyle change for you. Needless to say, the transition is not going to be smooth sailing, so having a clear reason helps you stick to the diet.

A lot of people who are following plant-based normally have the following reasons:

- Lowering the chance for chronic disease
- Managing their blood sugar level
- Reducing cholesterol
- Weight loss
- Increasing longevity
- Love for animals
- Love for the environment

There are many excellent reasons why you should start eating a plant-based diet. Follow whichever speaks to you. It should inspire and excite you. Consider writing down the purpose on a post-it note and stick it on the fridge, bathroom mirror, or anywhere that you would look at often or where you would need to resist temptations to revert to your old, unhealthy eating habits.

Cook Your Own Meals

Of course, many outlets offer plant-based food on their menu, but it is just better to prepare your own meals. There are two reasons why you want to prepare your own meals. For one, it is a lot cheaper than eating out. It might not look like much at a glance, but the number will add up a few months down the line. Another benefit is that you get to control what goes into the food and your body. Not all restaurants offer true plant-based foodstuffs. Some may have too much sugar. Others may contain a small amount of animal products.

Some may find it daunting to have to cook their own meals, but it is worth the effort. To make your life easier, you should cook your food for the whole week in advance. This requires planning, so spend some time on Saturday to think of what you need to cook and what you want to buy. From that, you have a grocery list and a purposeful shopping trip on Sunday. If you are unsure of what food to cook or what ingredients to buy, there are many online resources to help you get started.

If you know what you need to buy, the trip to the grocery store would not be difficult, even with all the temptations around you. If you need help, bring a friend or someone you trust to help control your urge when that bag of potato chips calls out to you.

With your weekly meal plan and all the ingredients on the table, it is time to do some preparation. Here, it is a matter of personal taste. Some just want to pre-wash and chop their veggies. Others go as far as to actually batch cook their weekly meal in advance so they don't have to spend any more time during the week to cook. How you approach food prep is up to you.

Learn More

This is also important. When you know more about health, nutrition, agriculture, environment, and animal welfare, it only fortifies your commitment and helps you stick to a plant-based diet. Sometimes, a new study may open the door to a new purpose for a plant-based diet for you. Again, there are many resources out there to help you gain a better understanding of the subject.

Diversify

One of the reasons people stop following a plant-based diet is it gets bland for them. So, once you start to feel comfortable or bored of following someone else's meal plans, consider putting together your own. You should have a clear idea of what food you want to include in your weekly meals. Else, consider picking up some new cookbooks. Alternatively, explore Pinterest, Instagram, and other vegan food blogs for some free recipes and inspirations.

Focus on Progress

Although this should be obvious, some people want to have a perfect run and expect to see no stumbling blocks along their journey. If they mess up somewhere, they just give up completely. In fact, many people in the plant-based diet community will admit that they sometimes revert to eating unhealthily once in a while, although they feel guilty about it. Mistakes tend to happen. It is no big deal. What is important is that you don't give up and continue pushing forward.

Never give up on your weeks' or months' worth of progress just because of a simple failure. That is how we all learn and grow, after all. What is important is not how many times you mess up. What matters is consistency. So long as you are making progress, it is a win for you, no matter how small or big.

What Transition Looks Like

If you feel intimidated about the whole thing, maybe because you don't know where to start. Considering how many foodstuffs you need to cut out of your life, it is no wonder why many people feel lost at this stage. Below is a rough map of what you should do to have a smooth transition into a plant-based diet. Keep in mind that it can take anywhere between 2 weeks to a month for each step.

First, start adding more plants. Instead of cutting out meat outright, consider incorporating more plants into your diet first. For instance, if you have scrambled eggs for breakfast, consider adding onions, mushrooms, and spinach. This would also be an excellent time to explore some plant-based alternatives and create your own meal plans.

From there, start focusing on cutting down meat consumption. Your next goal would be to eat meat only once a week. Now would be a good time to start replacing your meat with plant-based alternatives. For instance, tofu serves as a good meat substitute.

The third step would be to cut out all meat from your diet, including fish. At this point, you should feel comfortable creating your own plant-based meal plan to suit your particular taste. This is also about the time when you feel that you are losing steam. If so, check in with your why again to reinvigorate your commitment.

The next step would be to cut down on dairy products. It is actually easier than you think since there are also plant-based substitutes out there. Start by cutting out milk, then yogurt, then cheese. The final stage in this step would be to cut out the small things like cream, cheese sauce, whipped cream, and sour cream. You may need to spend a month on this before you can start to cut out dairy from your diet altogether.

The last step is to reduce and eliminate your egg intake. Hopefully, you have already been experimenting with ways to replace eggs in your diet by this point. In baking, flax eggs, chia eggs, applesauce, etc., are good alternatives to eggs. Start to use fewer eggs in your diet and eliminate it from your diet completely when you are ready.

Holidays and Social Events

Transitioning to a plant-based diet may put you in the spotlight as "that person" in a social gathering that offers many animal products. If all your friends aren't on a plant-based diet, you will definitely stand out. That said, it does not mean you have to concede and consume animal products for just that occasion. There are some strategies to navigate such social situations.

1. Put more emphasis on socializing: Social gatherings aren't all about eating. Otherwise, it wouldn't be called a social gathering. Many people missed this point and stress over what they should eat or what others would think about them. Maybe you are worried about people telling you that you can't eat something when you reveal that you are on a plant-based diet. In truth, you can eat anything you want. You just choose not to eat the things you don't want to. There is nothing to stress about here as no one can and should make you feel bad about your dietary choices. Instead of focusing on the food, turn your attention to socializing and enjoy the time hanging out with other people. You can always drink water and tea. You can catch up on food when you're home.
2. Bring your own food: This is a win-win strategy. You can show up with a vegan appetizer or dessert to a party. This has the benefit of keeping your stomach busy and proving a point. For one, you get to keep yourself relatively full during

the whole event. Moreover, you can share this with other people present to show them that you don't have to give up delicious food in the pursuit of health.
3. Ask the host: If you really are worried about whether there will be veggie-friendly options, consider reaching out to the host about it. Nowadays, people are very forgiving and accommodating about dietary diversity, so they may even be willing to prepare some plant-based foods for you or allow you to bring some yourself.
4. Plant-based snacks: Plant-based diet isn't only restricted to breakfast, lunch, or dinner. When snacking, consider stocking up with nuts, hummus, chips, and other plant-based snacks. Just make sure they don't contain undesirable ingredients such as too much salt if you buy them from the store.
5. Handling the naysayers: An environment that does not really support the idea of eating healthy can be daunting for plant-based eaters, ethical vegans, or anyone just trying to improve their health. They make it so easy to stray off the path and return to the old ways of eating unhealthy. This is why you should cook your own food. In a social gathering, people may start asking you about why you are doing this in the first place. In such a case, you can engage them as if they are intrigued by the subject. If it turns out that they are not interested and want to undermine your effort, just make a joke and change the subject. This is definitely not comfortable to do, but you get used to it over time.
6. Review your motivation: When the going gets tough, review your goals and motivation. It helps to remind you why you are going through with this in the first place. With a goal that really speaks to you, you can renew your motivation to continue as if you just start out.
7. Eat before you go: This is also a viable strategy. Unless you are going to a dinner party, having a meal before attending a social gathering is very useful as you can focus on socializing and not have to worry about what food is on the table.

CHAPTER 5: HOW TO EAT FOR HEALTHY AGING ON A PLANT-BASED DIET

Easing your way into a plant-based diet can be difficult, considering what you have to stop eating. In this chapter, we will discuss how you can start a plant-based diet without feeling too overwhelmed by the whole process if you don't want to follow the action plan we've outlined above.

A Meal a Day

Start with just a meal a day. More often than not, quitting cold turkey will not help. Sure, you might think it is the fastest way to get all the benefits of a plant-based diet. The problem here is that many people fail to maintain that over time. You want to make it as easy for yourself as possible, so starting slow is a viable strategy.

Once you get comfortable enough, your goal should be to make 50% of your meal comprising primarily of veggies. This serves as a nutritional safety net of sorts as they ensure that your body gets all the nutrients it needs.

Consider Plant-Based Variant

There is a vegan-friendly substitution to virtually every animal product on the market in this day and age. So, you can enjoy your favorite food, minus the animal product. Taste-wise, the difference should be mostly negligible. Health-wise, substituting with vegan ingredients is already a huge step-up. For instance, tofu, walnut, or black beans do well as a meat substitution. Cashew cream can replace cheese.

Roast, not Boil

A common mistake with vegan foods is that people boil their veggies, making it taste bland. This doesn't help if you already miss the rich flavor of the meat. Instead, consider roasting your veggies for more flavor. That way, you are more inclined to add more veggies into your meal.

Go for Plant-Based Proteins

As you get older, you need to increase your protein intake to ensure optimal health. Meat is usually the main source of protein. Thankfully, there are many vegan options out there, so you don't have to stress much about your next source of protein. Also, consider varying your protein sources to keep things fresh.

Get Support

Having someone who is also going green with you makes the entire process easier as you can keep each other motivated to eat green and save the planet. If you don't know anyone who would keep you accountable, fret not. There are many online communities on various forums and social media that are dedicated to the vegan life. They can be your source of motivation and inspiration and are more than happy to welcome a new member to their community.

CHAPTER 6: PLANT-BASED DIET AND WEIGHT LOSS

It has been well established that a vegan diet is one of the best ways to manage your weight. Loading up all the nutrients into your body instead of processed food, excessive salt, and saturated fat would be much better for your body.

People say that all you have to do is to do it correctly, which is easier said than done. Many novice vegans think that going green is a way to lose some weight. Done incorrectly, and you might end up doing the opposite.

Losing weight is boiled down into a simple equation. You lose weight if you burn off more calories than you put into your body. This caloric deficiency would force the body to burn off the fat in the body to replenish itself.

If you have a weight problem by overeating junk food, you would still have a weight problem if you overeat healthy food. The point is that just because you eat vegan does not mean it is impossible to overeat. You can still put in too many calories in your body, making it impossible to lose weight, even when you eat healthily.

In fact, this is exactly what is happening in the vegan world right now. About a decade ago, eating vegan was all about veggies, fruits, legumes, nuts, seeds, spices, etc. Back then, vegan foods were not as popular as they are today, so people had no choice but to prepare their own food.

Nowadays, vegan food is readily available and affordable, thanks to the economy of scale. These convenient offerings may not be that healthy for you, but they are still better than junk food. Thanks to this convenience, vegan people start to eat more. There are now vegans who suffer from weight issues and high cholesterol, just like people who don't actually follow a plant-based diet.

With that said, if you are experiencing weight problems, perhaps you have done one of the things below.

You are Not Eating Mostly Healthy Foods

One of the things that vegans struggle with is getting enough nutrients. They may stress over the little details and try to meet that daily recommended intake for every single nutrient or vitamin that they can find. This would often lead them to eat some food that is not entirely healthy for them just because they need that nutrient fix.

In reality, these things do not matter all that much. This is because, with all the veggies, fruits, whole grains, nuts, seeds, herbs, spices, and mushrooms to choose from, you have virtually endless combinations of what food you can prepare. In most cases, what you manage to put together provide your body with enough nutrients. What is important here is that you need to eat foods that are the least processed, as much as possible.

If you are worried about your weight, consider eating more whole plant foods rich in nutrients while still being calorically light, such as water-rich fruits and veggies. That way, you would feel full without overeating.

Moreover, suppose you are still concerned that you are not getting enough nutrients. In that case, there are supplements you can take to make up for that deficiency.

Health Halos

Remember that just because something is labeled vegan does not mean it is 100% healthy for your body. You start to see such labels in grocery shops and restaurant menus more and more frequently nowadays.

For one, it could be fake marketing, and that the food itself is actually not any different than the non-vegan variant. They may trick you into thinking that their vegan alternative is healthy for you and that they would charge you more for it.

On the other hand, the belief that vegan food is "healthier" than their non-vegan counterpart is not appropriately clarified. No matter how much you polish a stone, it will not be as shiny or expensive as a diamond. Some vegan food is still not that good for your body.

Take ice-cream, for example. No matter how you look at it, it is still ice-cream. Sure, the vegan variant might be healthier. If ice-cream scores 3/10 on a healthy food scale, vegan ice-cream scores 4 or 5/10. Both types of ice-cream still pack a fair amount of carbs, saturated fat, and sugar, so they aren't filling at all. An excellent alternative to ice-cream would be something like a cup of fruits and a glass of almond milk or yogurt.

Portions

This highlights the importance of following a meal plan with proper portions. Some people may eat vegan food, but they think that they don't have to measure their portions. The number may be minuscule, but it quickly adds up since it is easy for portions to get progressively larger, and we wouldn't even notice it.

For instance, a tablespoon of walnuts on your oatmeal for breakfast is fine. But eventually, you may start to add up to a handful or a half a cup. This little change introduces 200 calories into your body. That measly 200 calories can be the difference between calorie deficiency (weight loss) or calorie surplus (weight gain). Keep this up for a year, and you might put on 20 pounds of weight.

This is why some people prefer preparing a week's worth of food and portioning it properly in advance. That way, they don't have to worry about portioning since they know that whatever they grab is just the right serving size.

The most common culprit of weight gain here would be the small things that pack a lot of calories, such as nuts, seeds, and oil. So, if you have to use these in your food, make sure to use measuring spoons and cups. Otherwise, consider eating smaller servings.

Carbs

This is common for those who transition from a low diet carbs before they go vegan. It might be refreshing for them to have carbs on the plate again, but it becomes easy to get carried away. For instance, cereal for breakfast, a vegan pizza for lunch, and pasta with veggies for dinner, and maybe some whole-grain crackers as snacks throughout the day. This is a vegan diet that is full of carbs that the body does not need. So what does it do? It stores the excess carbs as fat, leading to weight gain again.

To circumvent this problem, make veggies the main component of your diet. You can also go for pasta, cereals, bread, and whole wheat since they are digested slowly. They force your body to burn more energy to digest them.

Not Eating Enough

Not eating enough food can actually lead to weight gain. This is because our body has a power-saving mode that will activate when it thinks that food will be scarce for some time in the future. This trigger can happen when you don't eat enough. What the body does is slow down metabolism so that you don't burn as much energy, allowing you to survive for a long time. This is a handy evolutionary feature, but it has some downsides.

The body will make sure that you get the message. That means you would always be hungry. Your body will burn calories much more slowly to save energy, but it will hold on to every calorie you put into it. This leads to calories surplus even though you don't eat enough.

Also, the hunger may set you up for a long streak of binge-eating food, vegan or not, which introduces more and more calories into your body. Your body will continue to do this until it thinks that food is no longer scarce before it vamps up metabolism to a normal rate again. By then, you would have already gained weight.

So, try to eat well-rounded, plant-based whole foodstuff rich in fiber, healthy fats, protein, and carbs. That way, you get all the nutrition, feel full, and keep that metabolism steady.

CHAPTER 7: OTHER HEALTHY HABITS

Keeping your body thin and your mind fresh takes more than just changing your diet. Suppose you only consume a plant-based diet without improving other habits. In that case, you will find that it gets increasingly difficult the further you go, not to mention that your health may not improve by that much. As such, you must pick up other healthy habits that complement your eating habits to amplify their benefits. Below are some ideas to help you get started.

Drink More Water

Staying hydrated is critical, even more so than eating healthy. You can't just drink a can of coke alongside your salad and expect to be healthy, however. For example, coffee and tea are fine so long as they don't contain sugar, milk, or cream.

Water is your best option. Half a glass or a glass of water before every meal ensures that you feel full faster, therefore eat less food. A glass of water first thing in the morning is powerful as your body hadn't had any water for 8 hours, assuming you sleep for 8 hours. Have a glass of water whenever you feel thirsty or between short breaks during your work. It goes a long way in keeping your mind and body energized.

Meditate

Meditation helps calm the mind and body. Numerous studies show that meditation has profound effects on both the body and mind. In fact, you do not even need to do much to get some of those benefits.

For example, a 5-minute meditation in the morning helps wake the body up. You will notice this effect when you take a deep breath soon after waking up. You can also do a 5-minute meditation right before bed to relax your mind and body before you sleep. It helps you get a more restful sleep.

Moreover, meditation helps slow down your mind and allow you to appreciate the simple things in life. You don't have to get any fancy gear or app for this. Sitting down and breathe deeply with your eyes closed for a few minutes is often enough for most people. However, if you want to delve deeper into this, there are many free resources online to help you get started, such as guided meditation videos and apps.

Exercise

They say that 70% of the weight loss is from the diet, and the other 30% is from exercise. That doesn't mean you should neglect exercising, however. You don't have to buy expensive gym equipment or get that membership that you won't use a few months down the line, either. A few simple exercises at home using your body as the weight are more than enough since you already have your plant-based diet doing most of the weight loss for you. Going for a jog, cycling, swimming regularly will make you feel better, look better, have more energy, sleep better, live longer, etc. The benefits of exercising are numerous, just like that of a plant-based diet.

Journal

Journaling isn't for everyone, but it helps you review your goals and visualize your success. Think of it, not as a chore where you have to write your own thoughts into a book. Instead, journaling should be a record of what you have learned about yourself, your feelings, etc. You don't have to do it every day if it is too much for you, but just have a habit of journaling from time to time.

Read

Reading for just 30 minutes a day helps a lot in improving yourself as a person. Besides, it provides a nice change of scenery from social media to something more intellectually stimulating. This habit goes well with a plant-based diet, as you can start by reading more about how it can help your health or the environment. There is always room for improvement, and a little bit of reading every day will add up a few years down the line.

Spend Time in Nature

Staying connected with nature is also essential. Going outside and spending some time in the park helps reconnect you to nature and reminds you of why you are going green in the first place. If you feel adventurous, you can also go camping, far away from the busy buzz of city life, and be with nature for a while.

Try Out New Things

Consider enriching your life by introducing fun, new activities. Do the things that you were initially reluctant to do, such as going bungee jumping, for instance. It'll be a new experience, and it will allow you to grow as a person.

Get Enough Sleep

Sleep is an important part of the equation when it comes to weight loss and improving your health as a whole. Sleep deprivation reduces your metabolism, which may lead to weight loss, among a whole host of other health problems. Also, it destroys your motivation to stick to your plant-based diet. A tired mind gives in easily to temptation, and you will find yourself reverting to eating junk food.

8 hours a day is recommended, or at least 7 hours. If you are really, really busy, you can get away with 6 hours, but only occasionally. If you go on for 6 hours of sleep or less every day, you will feel the fatigue settling in, and you will lose all motivation to do anything.

Also, it pays to have some sort of bedtime routine. It is a way of letting the body know that it is time to sleep. With enough repetition, the body will relax on its own as you go through this routine, and you can get a restful sleep.

A bedtime routine should be something that suits you. Some people prefer to have a quick shower before bed. Some like to read a book. Meditation works well here and should be incorporated into your bedtime routine.

One thing for sure, though, is that you must not stare at a screen before bed, especially social media. For one, the blue light will trick your brain into thinking that it is still day time and stops you from going to sleep. Another thing is that social media only makes you feel anxious, given how many people post stories of their success or other highlights of their life all the time. But they are just that – highlights. Spare yourself from the emotional turmoil and stay away from social media when it is close to bedtime so you can get a full sleep.

Connect with People

Also, you have your friends and family who would support you on this journey. Starting out on this journey can be difficult, and so having someone nearby for encouragement is always good. When starting out, you may be haunted by temptations to return to your old, unhealthy habits. Therefore, you can keep yourself busy with various activities and bonding with the people who love and care about you.

21-DAY MEAL PLAN

Day 1

Breakfast: Beans on Toast

Lunch: Brussels Sprout Skewers

Dinner: Mushroom Sliders

Dessert: Raspberry Muffins

Day 2

Breakfast: Grapes and Green Tea Smoothie

Lunch: Thai Peanut Butter Cauliflower Wings

Dinner: Lentil and Turnip Soup

Dessert: Chocolate Chip Cake

Day 3

Breakfast: Chickpea Flour Frittata
Lunch: Potato Salad
Dinner: Tomato and Chickpea Curry
Dessert: Coffee Cake

Day 4

Breakfast: Mango and Kale Smoothie
Lunch: Carrot Patties
Dinner: Lentil Stroganoff
Dessert: Chocolate Marble Cake

Day 5

Breakfast: Potato Pancakes
Lunch: Eggplant and Potatoes in Tomato Sauce
Dinner: Broccoli and Sun-dried Tomato Pasta
Dessert: Chocolate Chip Cookies

Day 6

Breakfast: Pomegranate Smoothie
Lunch: Grilled Mushrooms with Garlic Sauce
Dinner: Creamy Broccoli Pasta
Dessert: Lemon Cake

Day 7

Breakfast: Chocolate Chip Pancakes

Lunch: Sesame Tofu and Veggies Noodles

Dinner: Wild Rice Mushroom Soup

Dessert: Banana Muffins

Day 8

Breakfast: Coconut Water Smoothie

Lunch: Bombay Potatoes and Peas

Dinner: Kung Pao Lentils

Dessert: No-Bake Cookies

Day 9

Breakfast: Turmeric Steel-Cut Oats

Lunch: BBQ Tofu Pizza

Dinner: Orange Tofu

Dessert: Peanut Butter and Oat Bars

Day 10

Breakfast: Apple, Banana and Berry Smoothie

Lunch: Quinoa Tacos

Dinner: Lentil Brown Rice Soup

Dessert: Baked Apples

Day 11

Breakfast: Vegetable Pancakes

Lunch: Teriyaki Noodle Stir-Fry

Dinner: Peanut and Lentil Soup

Dessert: Chocolate Strawberry Shake

Day 12

Breakfast: Berry Ginger Zing Smoothie

Lunch: Garlicky Tofu

Dinner: Lentil with Spinach

Dessert: Chocolate Clusters

Day 13

Breakfast: Banana and Chia Pudding

Lunch: Mac and Cheese

Dinner: Lentil and Quinoa Loaf

Dessert: Banana Coconut Cookies

Day 14

Breakfast: Dragon Fruit Smoothie Bowl

Lunch: Peanut Butter and Pumpkin Soup

Dinner: Chorizo

Dessert: Chocolate Pots

Day 15

Breakfast: Tofu Scramble

Lunch: Sweet Korean Lentils

Dinner: Spiced Carrot and Millet Salad

Dessert: Maple and Tahini Fudge

Day 16

Breakfast: Chocolate Smoothie Bowl

Lunch: Pasta Puttanesca

Dinner: Carrots and Quinoa Veggie Bowl

Dessert: Creamsicles

Day 17

Breakfast: Pumpkin Spice Oatmeal

Lunch: Walnut Meat Tacos

Dinner: Pasta Primavera

Dessert: Peanut Butter, Nut and Fruit Cookies

Day 18

Breakfast: Zucchini and Blueberry Smoothie

Lunch: Couscous with Olives

Dinner: Chickpea Burgers

Dessert: Chocolate Covered Dates

Day 19

Breakfast: Peanut Butter Bites

Lunch: Black Bean and Corn Salad

Dinner: Wild Rice Soup

Dessert: Hot Chocolate

Day 20

Breakfast: Hot Pink Beet Smoothie

Lunch: Chickpea Salad Sandwich

Dinner: Sesame Cauliflower

Dessert: Vanilla Cupcakes

Day 21

Breakfast: Maple and Cinnamon Overnight Oats

Lunch: Ginger Veggie Stir-Fry

Dinner: Potato Curry

Dessert: Chockolate Mug Cake

BREAKFAST RECIPES

Grapes and Green Tea Smoothie

Prep Time: 5 minutes; Cooking Time: 0 minutes; Yields: 2 glasses;

Ingredients:

- ½ cup green tea
- ½ cup of green grapes
- 1 banana, peeled
- 1-inch piece of ginger
- ½ cup of ice cubes
- 2 cups baby spinach
- ½ of a medium apple, peeled, diced

Directions:

- Place all the ingredients into the jar of a high-speed food processor or blender in the order stated in the ingredients list and then cover it with the lid.
- Pulse for 1 minute until smooth, and then serve.

Nutritional Information per Serving:

Calories: 150 Cal; Fat: 2.5 g; Protein: 1 g; Carbs: 36.5 g; Fiber: 9 g;

Mango and Kale Smoothie

Prep Time: 5 minutes; Cooking Time: 0 minutes; Yields: 2 glasses;

Ingredients:

- 2 cups oats milk, unsweetened
- 2 bananas, peeled
- ½ cup kale leaves
- 2 teaspoons coconut sugar
- 1 cup mango pieces
- 1 teaspoon vanilla extract, unsweetened

Directions:

- Place all the ingredients into the jar of a high-speed food processor or blender in the order stated in the ingredients list and then cover it with the lid.
- Pulse for 1 minute until smooth, and then serve.

Nutritional Information per Serving:

Calories: 281 Cal; Fat: 3 g; Protein: 6 g; Carbs: 63 g; Fiber: 16 g;

Pomegranate Smoothie

Prep Time: 5 minutes; Cooking Time: 0 minutes; Yields: 2 glasses;

Ingredients:

- 2 cups almond milk, unsweetened

- 2 medium apples, cored, sliced
- 2 bananas, peeled
- 2 cups frozen raspberries
- 1 cup pomegranate seeds
- 4 teaspoons agave syrup

Directions:

- Place all the ingredients into the jar of a high-speed food processor or blender in the order stated in the ingredients list and then cover it with the lid.
- Pulse for 1 minute until smooth, and then serve.

Nutritional Information per Serving:

Calories: 141.5 Cal; Fat: 1.1 g; Protein: 4.1 g; Carbs: 30.8 g; Fiber: 2.4 g;

Coconut Water Smoothie

Prep Time: 5 minutes; Cooking Time: 0 minutes; Yields: 2 glasses;

Ingredients:

- 2 cups of coconut water
- 1 large apple, peeled, cored, diced
- 1 cup of frozen mango pieces
- 2 teaspoons peanut butter
- 4 teaspoons coconut flakes

Directions:

- Place all the ingredients into the jar of a high-speed food processor or blender in the order stated in the ingredients list and then cover it with the lid.

- Pulse for 1 minute until smooth, and then serve.

Nutritional Information per Serving:

Calories: 113.4 Cal; Fat: 0.3 g; Protein: 0.6 g; Carbs: 29 g; Fiber: 2 g;

Apple, Banana, and Berry Smoothie

Prep Time: 5 minutes; Cooking Time: 0 minutes; Yields: 2 glasses;

Ingredients:

- 2 cups almond milk, unsweetened
- 2 cups frozen strawberries
- 2 bananas, peeled
- 1 large apple, peeled, cored, diced
- 2 tablespoons peanut butter

Directions:

- Place all the ingredients into the jar of a high-speed food processor or blender in the order stated in the ingredients list and then cover it with the lid.
- Pulse for 1 minute until smooth, and then serve.

Nutritional Information per Serving:

Calories: 156.1 Cal; Fat: 3.2 g; Protein: 3 g; Carbs: 17 g; Fiber: 5.8 g;

Berry Ginger Zing Smoothie

Prep Time: 5 minutes; Cooking Time: 0 minutes; Yields: 2 glasses;

Ingredients:

- 2 cups almond milk, unsweetened
- 1 cup frozen raspberries
- 1 cup of frozen strawberries
- 1 cup cauliflower florets
- 2 1-inch pieces of ginger

Directions:

- Place all the ingredients into the jar of a high-speed food processor or blender in the order stated in the ingredients list and then cover it with the lid.
- Pulse for 1 minute until smooth, and then serve.

Nutritional Information per Serving:

Calories: 300 Cal; Fat: 8 g; Protein: 8 g; Carbs: 30 g; Fiber: 9 g;

Dragon Fruit Smoothie Bowl

Prep Time: 5 minutes; Cooking Time: 0 minutes; Yields: 2 bowls;

Ingredients:

For the Bowl:
- ½ cup coconut milk, unsweetened
- 2 bananas, peeled
- ½ cup frozen raspberries
- 7 ounces frozen dragon fruit
- 3 tablespoons vanilla protein powder

For the Toppings:
- 2 tablespoons coconut flakes
- 2 tablespoons hemp seeds

Directions:

- Place all the ingredients for the bowl into the jar of a high-speed food processor or blender in the order stated in the ingredients list and then cover it with the lid.
- Pulse for 1 minute until smooth, and then divide evenly between two bowls.
- Sprinkle 1 tablespoon of coconut flakes and hemp seeds over the smoothie and then serve.

Nutritional Information per Serving:

Calories: 225 Cal; Fat: 1.6 g; Protein: 8.1 g; Carbs: 48 g; Fiber: 8.9 g;

Chocolate Smoothie Bowl

Prep Time: 5 minutes; Cooking Time: 0 minutes; Yields: 2 bowls;

Ingredients:

For the Bowls:
- 2 cups almond milk, unsweetened
- 2 bananas, peeled
- 3 tablespoons cocoa powder
- 1 cup spinach leaves, fresh
- 2 tablespoons oat flour
- 4 Medjool dates, pitted
- 1/8 teaspoon salt
- 2 tablespoons vanilla protein powder
- 2 tablespoons peanut butter

For the Toppings:
- 2 tablespoons coconut flakes
- 2 tablespoons hemp seeds

Directions:

- Place all the ingredients for the bowl into the jar of a high-speed food processor or blender in the order stated in the ingredients list and then cover it with the lid.
- Pulse for 1 minute until smooth, and then divide evenly between two bowls.
- Sprinkle 1 tablespoon of coconut flakes and hemp seeds over the smoothie and then serve.

Nutritional Information per Serving:

Calories: 382 Cal; Fat: 14 g; Protein: 22 g; Carbs: 53 g; Fiber: 9 g;

Zucchini and Blueberry Smoothie

Prep Time: 5 minutes; Cooking Time: 0 minutes; Yields: 2 glasses;

Ingredients:

- 1 cup coconut milk, unsweetened
- 1 large celery stem
- 2 bananas, peeled
- ½ cup spinach leaves, fresh
- 1 cup frozen blueberries
- 2/3 cup sliced zucchini
- 1 tablespoon hemp seeds
- ½ teaspoon maca powder
- ¼ teaspoon ground cinnamon

Directions:

- Place all the ingredients into the jar of a high-speed food processor or blender in the order stated in the ingredients list and then cover it with the lid.
- Pulse for 1 minute until smooth, and then serve.

Nutritional Information per Serving:

Calories: 218 Cal; Fat: 10.1 g; Protein: 6.3 g; Carbs: 31.8 g; Fiber: 4.7 g;

Hot Pink Beet Smoothie

Prep Time: 5 minutes; Cooking Time: 0 minutes; Yields: 2 glasses;

Ingredients:

- 2 cups almond milk, unsweetened
- 2 clementine, peeled
- 1 cup raspberries
- 1 banana, peeled
- 1 medium beet, peeled, chopped
- 2 tablespoons chia seeds
- 1/8 teaspoon sea salt
- ½ teaspoon vanilla extract, unsweetened
- 4 tablespoons almond butter

Directions:

- Place all the ingredients into the jar of a high-speed food processor or blender in the order stated in the ingredients list and then cover it with the lid.
- Pulse for 1 minute until smooth, and then serve.

Nutritional Information per Serving:

Calories: 260.8 Cal; Fat: 1.3 g; Protein: 13 g; Carbs: 56 g; Fiber: 9.3 g;

Chickpea Flour Frittata

Prep Time: 10 minutes; Cooking Time: 50 minutes; Yields: 6 slices;

Ingredients:

- 1 medium green bell pepper, cored, chopped
- 1 cup chopped greens
- 1 cup cauliflower florets, chopped
- ½ cup chopped broccoli florets
- ½ of a medium red onion, peeled, chopped
- ¼ teaspoon salt
- ½ cup chopped zucchini

For the Batter:
- ¼ cup cashew cream
- 1 ½ cup chickpea flour
- ½ cup chopped cilantro
- ½ teaspoon salt
- ¼ teaspoon cayenne pepper
- ½ teaspoon dried dill
- ¼ teaspoon ground black pepper
- ¼ teaspoon dried thyme
- ½ teaspoon ground turmeric
- 1 tablespoon olive oil
- 1 ½ cup water

Directions:

- Switch on the oven, then set it to 375 degrees F and let it preheat.
- Take a 9-inch pie pan, grease it with oil, and then set aside until required.
- Take a large bowl, place all the vegetables in it, sprinkle with salt and then toss until combined.
- Prepare the batter and for this, add all of its ingredients in it except for thyme, dill, and cilantro and then pulse until combined and smooth.
- Pour the batter over the vegetables, add dill, thyme, and cilantro, and then stir until combined.

- Spoon the mixture into the prepared pan, spread evenly, and then bake for 45 to 50 minutes until done and inserted toothpick into frittata comes out clean.
- When done, let the frittata rest for 10 minutes, cut it into slices, and then serve.

Nutritional Information per Serving:

Calories: 153 Cal; Fat: 4 g; Protein: 7 g; Carbs: 20 g; Fiber: 4 g;

Potato Pancakes

Prep Time: 10 minutes; Cooking Time: 20 minutes; Yields: 10 pancakes;

Ingredients:

- ½ cup white whole-wheat flour
- 3 large potatoes, grated
- ½ of a medium white onion, peeled, grated
- 1 jalapeno, minced
- 2 green onions, chopped
- 1 tablespoon minced garlic
- 1 teaspoon salt
- ¼ teaspoon baking powder
- ¼ teaspoon ground pepper
- 4 tablespoons olive oil

Directions:

- Take a large bowl, place all the ingredients except for oil and then stir until well combined; stir in 1 to 2 tablespoons water if needed to mix the batter.
- Take a large skillet pan, place it over medium-high heat, add 2 tablespoons of oil and then let it heat.

- Scoop the pancake mixture in portions into the pan, shape each portion like a pancake and then cook for 5 to 7 minutes per side until pancakes turn golden brown and thoroughly cooked.
- When done, transfer the pancakes to a plate, add more oil into the pan and then cook more pancakes in the same manner.
- Serve straight away.

Nutritional Information per Serving:

Calories: 69 Cal; Fat: 1 g; Protein: 2 g; Carbs: 12 g; Fiber: 1 g;

Chocolate Chip Pancakes

Prep Time: 5 minutes; Cooking Time: 10 minutes; Yields: 6 pancakes;

Ingredients:

- 1 cup white whole-wheat flour
- ½ cup chocolate chips, vegan, unsweetened
- 1 tablespoon baking powder
- ¼ teaspoon salt
- 2 teaspoons coconut sugar
- 1 ½ teaspoon vanilla extract, unsweetened
- 1 cup almond milk, unsweetened
- 2 tablespoons coconut butter, melted
- 2 tablespoons olive oil

Directions:

- Take a large bowl, place all the ingredients except for oil and chocolate chips, and then stir until well combined.
- Add chocolate chips, and then fold until just mixed.

- Take a large skillet pan, place it over medium-high heat, add 1 tablespoon oil and then let it heat.
- Scoop the pancake mixture in portions into the pan, shape each portion like a pancake and then cook for 5 to 7 minutes per side until pancakes turn golden brown and thoroughly cooked.
- When done, transfer the pancakes to a plate, add more oil into the pan and then cook more pancakes in the same manner.
- Serve straight away.

Nutritional Information per Serving:

Calories: 172 Cal; Fat: 6 g; Protein: 2.5 g; Carbs: 28 g; Fiber: 8 g;

Turmeric Steel-Cut Oats

Prep Time: 5 minutes; Cooking Time: 10 minutes; Yields: 2 bowls;

Ingredients:

- ½ cup steel-cut oats
- 1/8 teaspoon salt
- 2 tablespoons maple syrup
- ½ teaspoon ground cinnamon
- 1/3 teaspoon turmeric powder
- ¼ teaspoon ground cardamom
- ¼ teaspoon olive oil
- 1 ½ cups water
- 1 cup almond milk, unsweetened

For the Topping:
- 2 tablespoons pumpkin seeds
- 2 tablespoons chia seeds

Directions:

- Take a medium saucepan, place it over medium heat, add oats, and then cook for 2 minutes until toasted.
- Pour in the milk and water, stir until mixed, and then bring the oats to a boil.
- Then switch heat to medium-low level, simmer the oats for 10 minutes, and add salt, maple syrup, and all spices.
- Stir until combined, cook the oats for 7 minutes or more until cooked to the desired level and when done, let the oats rest for 15 minutes.
- When done, divide oats evenly between two bowls, top with pumpkin seeds and chia seeds and then serve.

Nutritional Information per Serving:

Calories: 234 Cal; Fat: 4 g; Protein: 7 g; Carbs: 41 g; Fiber: 5 g;

Vegetable Pancakes

Prep Time: 10 minutes; Cooking Time: 20 minutes; Yields: 10 Pancakes;

Ingredients:

- 1/3 cup cooked and mashed sweet potato
- 2 cups grated carrots
- 1 cup chopped coriander
- 1 cup cooked spinach
- 3.5 ounces chickpea flour
- ½ teaspoon baking powder
- 1 ½ teaspoon salt
- 1 teaspoon ground turmeric
- 2 tablespoons olive oil
- ¾ cup of water

Directions:

- Take a large bowl, place chickpea flour in it, add turmeric powder, baking powder, and salt, and then stir until combined.
- Whisk in the water until combined, stir in sweet potatoes until well mixed and then add carrots, spinach, and coriander until well combined.
- Take a large skillet pan, place it over medium-high heat, add 1 tablespoon oil and then let it heat.
- Scoop the pancake mixture in portions into the pan, shape each portion like a pancake and then cook for 3 to 5 minutes per side until pancakes turn golden brown and thoroughly cooked.
- When done, transfer the pancakes to a plate, add more oil into the pan and then cook more pancakes in the same manner.
- Serve straight away.

Nutritional Information per Serving:

Calories: 74 Cal; Fat: 0.3 g; Protein: 3 g; Carbs: 16 g; Fiber: 2.7 g;

Banana and Chia Pudding

Prep Time: 25 minutes; Cooking Time: 12 minutes; Yields: 2 bowls;

Ingredients:

For the Pudding:
- 2 bananas, peeled
- 4 tablespoons chia seeds
- 2 tablespoons coconut sugar
- ½ teaspoon pumpkin pie spice
- 1/8 teaspoon sea salt
- 1 ½ cup almond milk, unsweetened

For the Bananas:

- 2 bananas, peeled, sliced
- 2 tablespoons coconut flakes
- 1/8 teaspoon ground cinnamon
- 2 tablespoons coconut sugar
- ¼ cup chopped walnuts
- 2 tablespoons almond milk, unsweetened

Directions:

- Prepare the pudding and for this, place all of its ingredients in a blender except for chia seeds and then pulse until smooth.
- Pour the mixture into a medium saucepan, place it over medium heat, bring the mixture to a boil and then remove the pan from heat.
- Add chia seeds into the hot banana mixture, stir until mixed, and then let it sit for 5 minutes.
- Whisk the pudding and then let it chill for 15 minutes in the refrigerator.
- Meanwhile, prepare the caramelized bananas and for this, take a medium skillet pan, and place it over medium heat.
- Add banana slices, sprinkle with salt, sugar, and nutmeg, drizzle with milk and then cook for 5 minutes until mixture has thickened.
- Assemble the pudding and for this, divide the pudding evenly between two bowls, top with banana slices, sprinkle with walnuts, and then serve.

Nutritional Information per Serving:

Calories: 495 Cal; Fat: 21 g; Protein: 9 g; Carbs: 76 g; Fiber: 14 g;

Tofu Scramble

Prep Time: 5 minutes; Cooking Time: 15 minutes; Yields: 3 plates;

Ingredients:

- 12 ounces tofu, extra-firm, pressed, drained
- ½ of a medium red onion, peeled, sliced
- 1 cup baby greens mix
- 1 medium red bell pepper, cored, sliced
- ½ teaspoon garlic powder
- 1 teaspoon salt
- ½ teaspoon ground black pepper
- ¼ teaspoon turmeric powder
- ¼ teaspoon ground cumin
- 4 tablespoons olive oil, divided

Directions:

- Take a large bowl, place tofu in it, and then break it into bite-size pieces.
- Add salt, black pepper, turmeric, and 2 tablespoons of oil, and then stir until mixed.
- Take a medium skillet pan, place it over medium heat, add garlic powder and cumin and then cook for 1 minute until fragrant.
- Add tofu mixture, stir until mixed, switch heat to medium-high level, and then cook for 5 minutes until tofu turn golden brown.
- When done, divide tofu evenly between three plates, keep it warm, and then set aside until required.
- Return the skillet pan over medium-high heat, add remaining oil and let it heat until hot.
- Add onion and bell peppers, cook for 5 to 7 minutes or until beginning to brown, and then season with a pinch of salt.
- Add baby greens, toss until mixed, and then cook for 30 seconds until leaves begin to wilts.
- Add vegetables evenly to the plates to scrambled tofu and then serve.

Nutritional Information per Serving:

Calories: 304 Cal; Fat: 25.6 g; Protein: 14.2 g; Carbs: 6.6 g; Fiber: 2.6 g;

Pumpkin Spice Oatmeal

Prep Time: 5 minutes; Cooking Time: 8 minutes; Yields: 2 Bowls;

Ingredients:

- ¼ cup Medjool dates, pitted, chopped
- 2/3 cup rolled oats
- 1 tablespoon maple syrup
- ½ teaspoon pumpkin pie spice
- ½ teaspoon vanilla extract, unsweetened
- 1/3 cup pumpkin puree
- 2 tablespoons chopped pecans
- 1 cup almond milk, unsweetened

Directions:

- Take a medium pot, place it over medium heat, and then add all the ingredients except for pecans and maple syrup.
- Stir all the ingredients until combined, and then cook for 5 minutes until the oatmeal has absorbed all the liquid and thickened to the desired level.
- When done, divide oatmeal evenly between two bowls, top with pecans, drizzle with maple syrup and then serve.

Nutritional Information per Serving:

Calories: 175 Cal; Fat: 3.2 g; Protein: 5.8 g; Carbs: 33 g; Fiber: 6.1 g;

Peanut Butter Bites

Prep Time: 10 minutes; Cooking Time: 0 minutes; Yields: 20 balls;

Ingredients:

- 1 cup rolled oats
- 12 Medjool dates, pitted
- ½ cup peanut butter, sugar-free

Directions:

- Plug in a blender or a food processor, add all the ingredients in its jar, and then cover with the lid.
- Pulse for 5 minutes until well combined, and then tip the mixture into a shallow dish.
- Shape the mixture into 20 balls, 1 tablespoon of mixture per ball, and then serve.

Nutritional Information per Serving:

Calories: 103.1 Cal; Fat: 4.3 g; Protein: 2.3 g; Carbs: 15.4 g; Fiber: 0.8 g;

Maple and Cinnamon Overnight Oats

Prep Time: 2 hours and 10 minutes; Cooking Time: 0 minutes; Yields: 4 bowls;

Ingredients:

- 2 cups rolled oats
- ¼ cup chopped pecans
- ¾ teaspoon ground cinnamon
- 1 teaspoon vanilla extract, unsweetened
- 3 tablespoons coconut sugar
- 3 tablespoons maple syrup
- 2 cups almond milk, unsweetened

Directions:

- Take four mason jars, and then oats, vanilla, and milk.
- Take a small bowl, add maple syrup, cinnamon, and sugar, stir until mixed, add this mixture into the oats mixture and then stir until combined.
- Cover the jars with the lid and then let them rest in the refrigerator for a minimum of 2 hours or more until thickened.
- When ready to eat, top the oats with pecans, sprinkle with cinnamon, drizzle with maple syrup and then serve.

Nutritional Information per Serving:

Calories: 292 Cal; Fat: 9 g; Protein: 7 g; Carbs: 48 g; Fiber: 6 g;

Beans on Toast

Prep Time: 5 minutes; Cooking Time: 10 minutes; Yields: 4 toasts;

Ingredients:

- 2 cups cooked navy beans
- 1/3 cup sun-dried tomatoes, chopped
- ½ of a medium white onion, peeled, chopped
- 1 teaspoon minced garlic
- 1 tablespoon molasses
- 2 teaspoons soy sauce
- ¼ cup tomato paste
- ¼ cup ketchup
- ¼ teaspoon liquid smoke
- 1 tablespoon olive oil
- ¼ cup of water
- 4 slices of whole-wheat bread

Directions:

- Take a large skillet pan, place it over medium-high heat, add oil and then let it heat.
- Add onion, stir in garlic and then cook for 5 minutes until onion begins to brown.
- Add remaining ingredients except bread slices, stir until combined, and then cook the mixture for 5 minutes or more until thoroughly hot.
- Spread the bean mixture over the bread slices and then serve.

Nutritional Information per Serving:

Calories: 290 Cal; Fat: 6 g; Protein: 9 g; Carbs: 51 g; Fiber: 2 g;

LUNCH RECIPES

Brussels Sprout Skewers

Prep Time: 10 minutes; Cooking Time: 20 minutes; Yields: 4;

Ingredients:

- ½ of a medium red onion, peeled, sliced into 1-inch squares
- 1 pound Brussels sprouts, halved
- ¼ teaspoon of sea salt
- 1 tablespoon maple syrup
- 3 tablespoons balsamic vinegar
- 1 tablespoon Dijon mustard
- 3 tablespoons olive oil

Directions:

- Take a large pot half full with water, place it over medium-high heat and then bring it to a boil.
- Add Brussel sprouts, cook for 1 minute until tender, remove them from the pot, rinse well until cold water and then pat dry with paper towels.
- Transfer Brussel sprouts in a large bowl, add onion and remaining ingredients, and then toss until coated.

- Take a griddle pan, place it over medium-high heat, grease it with oil and then let it heat until hot.
- Thread Brussel sprouts and onions on skewers, four sprouts per skewer, and then brush with remaining marinade.
- Arrange the prepared skewers onto the grill pan and then cook for 7 to 10 minutes per side until vegetables turn nicely brown.
- Serve straight away.

Nutritional Information per Serving:

Calories: 159.3 Cal; Fat: 10.5 g; Protein: 3.9 g; Carbs: 13.2 g; Fiber: 4.5 g;

Thai Peanut Butter Cauliflower Wings

Prep Time: 15 minutes; Cooking Time: 30 minutes; Yields: 4;

Ingredients:

- ½ of large head cauliflower, cut into florets
- 1 tablespoon minced Thai chili
- ½ teaspoon ginger powder
- 1 cup panko breadcrumbs
- 2 tablespoons lime juice
- 2 teaspoons soy sauce
- ½ cup peanut butter
- ¼ cup of water

Directions:

- Switch on the oven, then set it to 400 degrees F and let it preheat.
- Meanwhile, take a medium bowl, add ginger, minced chili, peanut butter, water, lime juice, and soy sauce and then whisk until smooth.
- Take a shallow dish and then spread panko breadcrumbs in it.

- Working on cauliflower florets at a time, dip into the peanut butter mixture, coat in breadcrumbs, and then place on a baking sheet lined with parchment sheet.
- Spray oil over the cauliflower florets and then bake for 30 minutes until florets turn crisp, turning halfway.
- Serve straight away.

Nutritional Information per Serving:

Calories: 130 Cal; Fat: 4 g; Protein: 4 g; Carbs: 19 g; Fiber: 2 g;

Potato Salad

Prep Time: 45 minutes; Cooking Time: 45 minutes; Yields: 6;

Ingredients:

- 2.8-pound potatoes
- 1 cup chopped dill pickles
- 23 ounces cooked peas
- 3 tablespoons chopped dill
- ¾ teaspoon salt
- 1 tablespoon coconut sugar
- ½ teaspoon ground black pepper
- 2 ¼ cup mayonnaise, plant-based

Directions:

- Rinse the potatoes, place them in a large pot, and then pour in enough water until potatoes are covered by 1-inch.
- Place the pot over medium-high heat and then cook for 20 to 30 minutes until tender.
- When done, drain the potatoes and let them cool for 15 minutes.

- Meanwhile, take a large bowl, place mayonnaise in it, add sugar, salt, and black pepper and then whisk until combined.
- Peel the cooled potatoes, cut them into small pieces, add to the mayonnaise mixture along with peas, pickles, and dill and then mix until thoroughly coated.
- Let the salad in the refrigerator for 30 minutes until chilled and then serve.

Nutritional Information per Serving:

Calories: 178.9 Cal; Fat: 5.1 g; Protein: 4.2 g; Carbs: 31.4 g; Fiber: 10.1 g;

Carrot Patties

Prep Time: 10 minutes; Cooking Time: 15 minutes; Yields: 15 patties;

Ingredients:

- 14 ounces cooked white beans
- 2 cups grated carrots
- 1 medium white onion, peeled, chopped
- ½ cup white whole-wheat flour
- ½ teaspoon curry powder
- ¾ teaspoon dried rosemary
- 1 teaspoon salt
- ¾ teaspoon dried thyme
- ½ teaspoon cumin powder
- 2 tablespoons olive oil

Directions:

- Take a large bowl, place beans in it, and then mash with a fork.
- Add remaining ingredients except for oil, stir until well combined, and then shape the mixture into fifteen patties.
- Take a large skillet pan, place it over medium-high heat, add oil and then let it heat.

- Arrange the prepared patties in the pan and then cook for 2 to 3 minutes per side until golden brown and thoroughly cooked.
- Serve straight away.

Nutritional Information per Serving:

Calories: 96 Cal; Fat: 5 g; Protein: 2.6 g; Carbs: 12.2 g; Fiber: 3.1 g;

Eggplant and Potatoes in Tomato Sauce

Prep Time: 5 minutes; Cooking Time: 15 minutes; Yields: 4;

Ingredients:

- 3 large potatoes, boiled, sliced
- 14 ounces crushed tomatoes
- 1 medium eggplant, destemmed, sliced
- 2 tablespoons minced garlic
- 1 teaspoon salt
- 1 tablespoon curry powder
- 1 tablespoon soy sauce
- 3 tablespoons olive oil

Directions:

- Take a large skillet pan, place it over medium heat, add oil, and let it heat.
- Add eggplant pieces, stir until coated, and then cook for 5 minutes until golden brown.
- Add garlic, season with salt and curry powder, cook for 1 minute and then stir in tomatoes.
- Cover the skillet pan with its lid and then simmer the vegetables for 7 minutes until thoroughly cooked.
- Add potato cubes, drizzle with soy sauce, stir until well combined, and then cook for 1 to 2 minutes until thoroughly hot.

- Serve straight away.

Nutritional Information per Serving:

Calories: 76 Cal; Fat: 0.5 g; Protein: 2.5 g; Carbs: 18.3 g; Fiber: 4.4 g;

Grilled Mushrooms with Garlic Sauce

Prep Time: 10 minutes; Cooking Time: 30 minutes; Yields: 2;

Ingredients:

- 2 large Portobello mushrooms

For the Marinade:
- 1 tablespoon minced garlic
- 1/3 teaspoon salt
- ¾ teaspoon smoked paprika
- 1/3 teaspoon ground black pepper
- 2 tablespoons balsamic vinegar
- 2 teaspoons lemon juice
- 2 teaspoons soy sauce
- 1 teaspoon white wine vinegar
- 1 teaspoon olive oil

For the Garlic Sauce:
- ¼ cup cashews
- 1 medium white onion, peeled, chopped
- 4 teaspoons minced garlic
- ½ teaspoon salt
- 1 tablespoon arrowroot powder
- 1 tablespoon nutritional yeast
- 1 tablespoon lemon juice
- 2 tablespoons white wine
- 1 teaspoon and 1 tablespoon olive oil
- 1 ½ cup water

Directions:

- Switch on the oven, then set it to 400 degrees F and let it preheat.
- Meanwhile, prepare the marinade and for this, take a shallow dish, place all the ingredients in it and then stir until well combined.
- Add mushrooms into the marinade dish, toss until well coated, and then let them marinate for 15 minutes.
- Arrange the mushrooms on a baking sheet lined with foil and then bake for 30 minutes until tender.
- Meanwhile, prepare the garlic sauce and for this, take a medium skillet pan, place it over medium heat, add 1 teaspoon oil and let it heat until hot.
- Add onion and garlic, cook for 5 minutes until tender, and then transfer half of this mixture into a food processor or blender.
- Add remaining ingredients for the sauce in it, cover with the lid, and then pulse for 1 minute or more until well combined.
- Spoon the mixture into the skillet pan, stir until mixed with the remaining onion mixture and then cook for 4 to 6 minutes until thickened to the desired level.
- When the mushrooms have baked, divide them evenly among plates, drizzle with the garlic sauce and then serve.

Nutritional Information per Serving:

Calories: 198 Cal; Fat: 12 g; Protein: 5 g; Carbs: 17.8 g; Fiber: 2 g;

Sesame Tofu and Veggies Noodles

Prep Time: 10 minutes; Cooking Time: 30 minutes; Yields: 3;

Ingredients:

For the Noodles:
- 6 ounces brown rice noodles
- 1 teaspoon lemon juice
- ½ teaspoon sesame oil
- ¼ teaspoon red pepper flakes

For the Sesame Tofu:
- 14 ounces tofu, extra-firm, pressed, drained, cut into cubes
- 1 cup of mixed vegetables
- ½ of large red bell pepper, cored, sliced
- 1 hot green chile, chopped
- 1 large green bell pepper, cored, sliced
- ½ cup sliced carrots
- 2 tablespoons chopped garlic
- 1 tablespoon grated ginger
- 1 tablespoon cornstarch
- 1 teaspoon olive oil
- 2 teaspoons sesame oil
- ½ cup of water
- 1 teaspoon sesame seeds

For the Sauce:
- ¼ teaspoon salt
- 1/8 teaspoon ground black pepper
- ¼ cup maple syrup
- 1/3 cup soy sauce
- 3 teaspoons Sriracha sauce
- 3 tablespoons apple cider vinegar
- 1 tablespoon orange juice

Directions:

- Prepare the noodles by following the instructions on its package, rinse them under cold water, drain well, and then place them in a large bowl.

- Add remaining ingredients for the noodles in it, toss until combined, divide evenly among three bowls, and then set aside until required.
- Prepare the tofu and for this, take a large skillet pan, place it over medium heat, add olive oil and then let it heat until hot.
- Add tofu, cook for 2 to 3 minutes per side until golden brown and then transfer to a shallow dish.
- Add sesame oil into the pan, add green chile, bell pepper, and vegetables, toss until coated in oil, and then cook for 4 minutes until tender-crisp.
- Stir in ginger and garlic, cook for 3 minutes, add all the ingredients for the sauce, stir until mixed and cook for 1 minute.
- Return tofu pieces into the pan, toss until coated, bring the sauce to a rolling boil and cook for 3 minutes.
- Whisk together cornstarch and water, add to the sauce, stir until mixed, and then cook for 3 to 4 minutes until the sauce has thickened to the desired level.
- Spoon tofu and sauce over the noodles, sprinkle with sesame seeds, and then serve.

Nutritional Information per Serving:

Calories: 488 Cal; Fat: 9 g; Protein: 14.1 g; Carbs: 84 g; Fiber: 4 g;

Bombay Potatoes and Peas

Prep Time: 10 minutes; Cooking Time: 35 minutes; Yields: 3;

Ingredients:

- 3 medium potatoes, 1/2-inch cubed
- 1 small red onion, peeled, chopped
- 1 large tomato
- 1 cup cooked peas
- 2 tablespoons minced garlic

- 1-inch piece of ginger, grated
- ¾ teaspoon salt
- ½ teaspoon red chili powder
- ½ teaspoon cumin seeds
- 1 teaspoon ground coriander
- ½ teaspoon turmeric powder
- 1 teaspoon mustard seeds
- ½ teaspoon ground cumin
- ½ teaspoon garam masala
- 2 teaspoons olive oil
- 1 cup of water
- ¼ cup chopped cilantro

Directions:

- Take a large skillet pan, place it over medium heat, add oil and let it heat until hot.
- Add mustard and cumin seeds, cook for 1 to 2 minutes until golden brown and fragrant, then stir in onion and cook for 5 minutes.
- Meanwhile, cut tomatoes into pieces, add them into a blender, add ginger and garlic and then pulse until pureed.
- Pour the tomato mixture into the pan, add all the spices, stir until mixed, and then cook for 5 minutes until the tomato mixture has thickened to the desired level.
- Add potatoes, season with salt, pour in water, stir until mixed, cover the pan with its lid, and then cook for 10 minutes.
- Stir peas into the potato mixture, taste to adjust seasoning, switch heat to medium-low level and then continue simmering the vegetables for 10 to 12 minutes until potatoes turn tender.
- When done, garnish potatoes and peas with cilantro and then serve.

Nutritional Information per Serving:

Calories: 232.3 Cal; Fat: 3.9 g; Protein: 9.8 g; Carbs: 42.4 g; Fiber: 9.4 g;

BBQ Tofu Pizza

Prep Time: 25 minutes; Cooking Time: 15 minutes; Yields: 2;

Ingredients:

For the Crust:
- ¾ cup spelt flour
- 2 teaspoons active yeast
- 1 tablespoon cornstarch
- 1/3 teaspoon salt
- 2 teaspoons olive oil
- 1 teaspoon maple syrup
- ¼ cup and 2 tablespoons hot water

For the Tofu:
- 1 cup tofu cubes, pressed, drained
- ½ teaspoon garlic powder
- 3 teaspoons Sriracha sauce
- 2 tablespoons BBQ sauce

For the Toppings:
- 1 medium red bell pepper, cored, sliced
- 1 medium red onion, peeled, sliced
- 2/3 cup marinara sauce
- 1 ½ cup shredded cashew cheese
- salt
- black pepper

Directions:

- Prepare the tofu and for this, take a large bowl, place tofu pieces in it, add remaining ingredients, toss until well coated, and then let the tofu rest until required.
- Prepare the crust and for this, take a small bowl, place maple syrup in it, add yeast, pour in the water, whisk until combined, and then let the mixture rest for 5 minutes until frothy.
- Take a large bowl, place flour in it, add yeast, cornstarch, and salt and then stir until combined.
- Add the yeast mixture into the flour mixture, add oil, stir until well combined, and then knead the mixture for 2 minutes until a smooth dough comes together.
- Transfer the dough onto the clean working surface dusted with flour, roll it into 12-inch wide round crust and then let it rest at a warm place for a minimum of 10 minutes.
- Meanwhile, switch on the oven, then set it to 450 degrees F and let it preheat.
- After 10 minutes, transfer the crust to a baking sheet, spread marinara sauce on it, and then scatter with red bell pepper pieces and onion slices.
- Sprinkle salt and black pepper over the vegetables, scatter tofu pieces on the crust, sprinkle cheese on top, and then bake for 12 to 15 minutes until thoroughly cooked.
- When done, let the pizza rest for 15 minutes, cut it into slices, and then serve.

Nutritional Information per Serving:

Calories: 394 Cal; Fat: 11 g; Protein: 15 g; Carbs: 55 g; Fiber: 9 g;

Quinoa Tacos

Prep Time: 10 minutes; Cooking Time: 35 minutes; Yields: 10 tacos;

Ingredients:

- ½ of medium red bell pepper, cored, sliced

- 1 cup quinoa
- ½ of medium orange bell pepper, cored, sliced
- 2 green onions
- 4 cups mixed greens
- 1 teaspoon onion powder
- 1 teaspoon garlic powder
- ½ teaspoon salt, divided
- 1 tablespoon cumin powder
- 1 teaspoon dried oregano
- 1 tablespoon paprika
- 3 tablespoons coconut oil
- 2 cups vegetable broth
- 2 tablespoons lime juice
- 12 tablespoons cashew cream
- 12 tablespoons salsa
- 12 corn tortillas

Directions:

- Cook the quinoa, and for this, take a medium saucepan, place it over medium heat and let it heat until hot.
- Add quinoa, cook for 3 to 4 minutes until toasted, transfer quinoa to a strainer, and then rinse it well.
- Return quinoa into the saucepan, pour in the vegetable broth, stir in ¼ teaspoon salt and then bring quinoa to boil.
- Switch heat to the low level, cover the pan with its lid and then simmer quinoa for 15 to 20 minutes until the quinoa has absorbed all the liquid.
- Meanwhile, take a medium bowl, place red bell pepper slices in it, drizzle with 1 tablespoon of lime juice, toss until coated, and then set aside until required.
- When done, remove the saucepan from heat, let the quinoa rest for 5 minutes, uncover the pan and then fluff with a fork.
- Take a large skillet pan, place it over medium heat, add oil and let it heat until melted.

- Add quinoa, stir until combined, stir in remaining salt, onion powder, garlic powder, cumin, and paprika and then cook for 5 minutes until bottom begins to turn crisp, don't stir.
- Remove pan from heat, add green onions and remaining lime juice, and stir until mixed.
- Assemble the tacos and for this, warm the tortillas until hot and slightly blacken and then fill evenly with mixed greens.
- Stuff the tortillas with quinoa mixture, red bell peppers, salsa, and cashew cream, and then serve.

Nutritional Information per Serving:

Calories: 150.5 Cal; Fat: 5.2 g; Protein: 4 g; Carbs: 23.3 g; Fiber: 3.5 g;

Teriyaki Noodle Stir-Fry

Prep Time: 15 minutes; Cooking Time: 15 minutes; Yields: 3;

Ingredients:

- 2 cups shredded cabbage
- 1 large red bell pepper, cored, sliced
- 2 medium carrots, julienned
- 4 button mushrooms, sliced
- 1 cup snow peas
- 1 teaspoon minced garlic
- 1 tablespoon olive oil
- 8 ounces of rice noodles
- 4 green onions, chopped

For the Sauce:
- ¼ cup of soy sauce
- 1 tablespoon coconut sugar
- 1 teaspoon apple cider vinegar
- ½ teaspoon sesame oil
- 1/8 teaspoon ground black pepper

Directions:

- Prepare the noodles and for this, take a large bowl, place noodles in it, cover with hot water and then let it rest for 10 minutes until tender.
- Meanwhile, prepare the sauce and for this, take a small bowl, place all of its ingredients in it, stir until well mixed, and then set aside until required.
- Then drain the noodles, rinse under cold water, and set aside until required.
- Take a large skillet pan, place it over medium-high heat, add oil and let it heat until hot.
- Add mushrooms, carrots, cabbage, and bell pepper, stir in garlic and then cook for 2 to 3 minutes until tender-crisp.
- Add green onions and snow peas, continue cooking for 1 minute, and then add noodles.
- Drizzle the prepared sauce over the noodles, toss until coated, switch heat to a high level, and then cook for 2 minutes until thoroughly hot.
- Toss until coated, and then serve.

Nutritional Information per Serving:

Calories: 302 Cal; Fat: 16.6 g; Protein: 4.1 g; Carbs: 27.8 g; Fiber: 3.3 g;

Garlicky Tofu

Prep Time: 5 minutes; Cooking Time: 15 minutes; Yields: 2;

Ingredients:

- 2 tablespoons cornstarch
- 14 ounces tofu, extra-firm, pressed, drained
- 1 tablespoon sesame oil

- 1 teaspoon sesame seeds

For The Sauce:
- 2 teaspoons cornstarch
- 2 teaspoons maple syrup
- ½ teaspoon apple cider vinegar
- ¼ cup of soy sauce
- 1 ½ teaspoon chili garlic sauce
- 2 tablespoons water

Directions:

- Take a large bowl, place tofu pieces in it, sprinkle with cornstarch, and then toss until coated.
- Prepare the sauce and for this, take a medium bowl, place all of its ingredients in it and then whisk until combined.
- Take a large skillet pan, place it over medium-high heat, add oil in it, and then let it heat until hot.
- Add tofu pieces, and then cook for 2 to 3 minutes per side until golden brown.
- Pour in the prepared sauce, toss until coated, and then cook for 3 to 4 minutes until the sauce has thickened to the desired level.
- Garnish the tofu with sesame seeds, and then serve.

Nutritional Information per Serving:

Calories: 313 Cal; Fat: 16 g; Protein: 19 g; Carbs: 17 g; Fiber: 7 g;

Mac and Cheese

Prep Time: 5 minutes; Cooking Time: 10 minutes; Yields: 2;

Ingredients:

- 1 cup pasta, uncooked
- 4 tablespoons nutritional yeast
- ½ teaspoon onion powder
- 1 teaspoon turmeric powder
- 1 teaspoon Dijon mustard
- 4 tablespoons ketchup
- 1 cup of water
- ½ cup carrot puree

Directions:

- Take a large heatproof bowl, place pasta in it, pour in water, and then stir until combined.
- Place the bowl into the microwave, cook it for 2 minutes, stir the pasta and then continue cooking it for 2 minutes or more until the pasta has absorbed all the liquid.
- Add remaining ingredients except for ketchup, stir until combined, and then continue microwaving for 3 minutes until hot.
- Top the pasta with ketchup and then serve.

Nutritional Information per Serving:

Calories: 270 Cal; Fat: 2 g; Protein: 11.6 g; Carbs: 52 g; Fiber: 8.2 g;

Peanut Butter and Pumpkin Soup

Prep Time: 5 minutes; Cooking Time: 12 minutes; Yields: 4;

Ingredients:

- 1 tablespoon Thai red curry paste
- 1 tablespoon agave syrup
- 2 tablespoons peanut butter
- 1 tablespoon soy sauce
- 1 tablespoon Sriracha sauce
- 2 cups vegetable broth

- ¼ cup coconut milk, unsweetened
- 1 2/3 cup pumpkin puree

Directions:

- Take a large pot, place it over medium-high heat and then let it heat until hot.
- Add curry paste into the pot, cook for 1 minute until fragrant, add remaining ingredients, and then whisk until combined.
- Cook the soup for 5 to 10 minutes until thoroughly hot and then serve.

Nutritional Information per Serving:

Calories: 132 Cal; Fat: 10 g; Protein: 3 g; Carbs: 8 g; Fiber: 2 g;

Sweet Korean Lentils

Prep Time: 5 minutes; Cooking Time: 10 minutes; Yields: 2;

Ingredients:

For the Lentils:
- 1 cup red lentils
- ½ of a medium white onion, peeled, chopped
- 2 green onions, chopped
- 1 tablespoon peanut oil
- 1 tablespoon sesame seeds

For the Sauce:
- 1 teaspoon minced garlic
- 3 tablespoons coconut sugar
- 1-inch piece of ginger, grated
- ½ teaspoon crushed red pepper flakes

- 1 teaspoon sesame oil
- ¼ cup of soy sauce
- 2 cups of water

Directions:

- Prepare the sauce and for this, take a medium bowl, place all of its ingredients in it and then whisk until combined.
- Take a large skillet pan, place it over medium heat, add oil and then let it heat until hot.
- Add onion, cook for 5 minutes until beginning to brown, add lentils, pour in the sauce, and then stir until mixed.
- Cover the pan with its lid, bring the lentils to simmer, and then cook for 8 to 10 minutes until lentils have turned tender and have absorbed most of the cooking liquid.
- When done, garnish lentils with green onions and sesame seeds and then serve.

Nutritional Information per Serving:

Calories: 253 Cal; Fat: 6 g; Protein: 13 g; Carbs: 36 g; Fiber: 14 g;

Pasta Puttanesca

Prep Time: 10 minutes; Cooking Time: 40 minutes; Yields: 4;

Ingredients:

- 28 ounces diced tomatoes
- ½ cup olives
- 2 teaspoons coconut sugar
- ¼ teaspoon salt
- ½ teaspoon red pepper flakes
- 2 teaspoons minced garlic
- 8 ounces pasta

- 1 tablespoon capers
- 1 tablespoon olive oil

Directions:

- Prepare the pasta, and for this, cook it according to the instructions on its package and then set aside until required.
- Take a large skillet pan, place it over medium-high heat, add oil and then let it heat until hot.
- Add olives, capers, and garlic, stir until mixed, and then cook for 2 minutes until garlic turns golden brown.
- Add tomatoes, stir in salt, red pepper flakes, and sugar, and then simmer the mixture for 25 to 30 minutes until thoroughly cooked.
- Add cooked pasta, toss until coated, and then cook for 2 to 3 minutes until hot.
- Serve straight away.

Nutritional Information per Serving:

Calories: 290 Cal; Fat: 7.5 g; Protein: 9.5 g; Carbs: 46.5 g; Fiber: 4.8 g;

Walnut Meat Tacos

Prep Time: 10 minutes; Cooking Time: 20 minutes; Yields: 8 tacos;

Ingredients:

For the Meat:
- ½ cup walnuts
- 6 sun-dried tomatoes
- 1 cup almonds
- ¼ teaspoon onion powder
- ¼ teaspoon garlic powder
- 1/3 teaspoon salt
- ¼ teaspoon ground black pepper
- ½ teaspoon paprika
- ¼ teaspoon cayenne pepper

For Serving:
- 8 taco shells
- 8 tablespoons salsa
- 8 tablespoons shredded cashew cheese

Directions:

- Switch on the oven, then set it to 350 degrees F and let it preheat.
- Take a medium bowl, place walnuts in it, cover with hot water, and then let it soak for 20 minutes.
- Take a separate medium bowl, place tomatoes in it, cover with hot water, and then let it soak for 20 minutes.
- After 20 minutes, drain the walnuts and tomatoes, and then place them in a food processor.
- Add remaining ingredients for the meat and then pulse until the crumbly mixture comes together.
- Spread the meat into a baking dish and then bake for 20 minutes until cooked.
- When done, spoon the meat evenly among taco shells, top each shell with 1 tablespoon of salsa and cashew cheese and then serve.

Nutritional Information per Serving:

Calories: 240 Cal; Fat: 23.7 g; Protein: 5.7 g; Carbs: 5.6 g; Fiber: 2.7 g;

Couscous with Olives

Prep Time: 5 minutes; Cooking Time: 30 minutes; Yields: 4;

Ingredients:

- ½ cup sliced black olives
- 1 medium shallot, peeled, minced
- 1/3 cup chopped sun-dried tomatoes

- 2 teaspoons minced garlic
- 5 tablespoons olive oil, divided
- 1 cup vegetable broth
- ½ cup pine nuts
- ¼ cup chopped parsley

For the Couscous:
- 2 cups couscous
- 1/8 teaspoon salt
- 1/8 teaspoon ground black pepper
- 1 ¼ cups vegetable broth
- 1 ¼ cups water

Directions:

- Prepare the couscous and for this, take a medium saucepan, place it over medium-high heat, add vegetable broth and water and then bring it to a boil.
- Add couscous, stir in salt and black pepper, switch heat to the low level, and then simmer the couscous for 8 minutes until it has absorbed all of its cooking liquid.
- When done, remove the pan from heat, let couscous rest for 5 minutes, fluff it with a fork and then let it rest until required.
- Take a large skillet pan, place it over medium-high heat, add 3 tablespoons of oil and then let it heat until hot.
- Take a separate saucepan, place it over medium heat, add the remaining oil, and then let it heat.
- Add shallot and garlic, cook for 2 minutes until shallot begins to turn tender, add tomatoes and olives, and then continue cooking for 3 minutes.
- Pour in the vegetable broth, bring the sauce to boil, then witch heat to a low level, and then simmer the sauce for 8 to 10 minutes until reduced by half.
- Take a large bowl, place couscous in it, add cooked sauce and stir until well combined.

- Top the couscous with parsley and pine nuts, and then serve.

Nutritional Information per Serving:

Calories: 527.7 Cal; Fat: 29.3 g; Protein: 13 g; Carbs: 55.5 g; Fiber: 5.4 g;

Black Bean and Corn Salad

Prep Time: 5 minutes; Cooking Time: 0 minutes; Yields: 6;

Ingredients:

- 30 ounces cooked black beans
- 1 large avocado, peeled, pitted, diced
- 1 ½ cups frozen corn kernels
- 1 large red bell pepper, cored, chopped
- 6 green onions, thinly sliced
- 2 large tomatoes, chopped
- ½ cup chopped cilantro

For the Salad Dressing:
- 1/3 cup lime juice
- ½ cup olive oil
- ½ teaspoon minced garlic
- 1 teaspoon salt
- ⅛ teaspoon ground cayenne pepper

Directions:

- Prepare the salad dressing, and for this, take a small jar, place all of its ingredients in it.
- Cover the jar with its lid, and then shake it well until mixed.
- Take a large salad bowl, place all the ingredients for the salad in it, and then pour the prepared salad dressing over it.
- Stir until well coated, and then serve the salad.

Nutritional Information per Serving:

Calories: 391 Cal; Fat: 24.5 g; Protein: 10.5 g; Carbs: 35.1 g; Fiber: 12.2 g;

Chickpea Salad Sandwich

Prep Time: 10 minutes; Cooking Time: 0 minutes; Yields: 2;

Ingredients:

- 1 1/2 cups cooked chickpeas
- 1 rib celery, sliced
- 1 cup mixed greens
- 3 green onions, sliced
- ½ teaspoon salt
- ½ teaspoon ground black pepper
- 1 teaspoon celery seed
- 1 tablespoon lemon juice
- 2 tablespoons cashew cream
- 4 slices of whole-wheat bread

Directions:

- Take a large bowl, place chickpeas in it, and then mash with a fork.
- Add remaining ingredients except for bread and then stir until well combined.
- Spread the salad evenly on top of two bread slices, cover the top with remaining bread slices, and then serve.

Nutritional Information per Serving:

Calories: 384 Cal; Fat: 12.2 g; Protein: 11.4 g; Carbs: 54.3 g; Fiber: 14 g;

Ginger Veggie Stir-Fry

Prep Time: 5 minutes; Cooking Time: 10 minutes; Yields: 6;

Ingredients:

- 1 small head of broccoli, cut into florets
- ¾ cup julienned carrots
- ¼ cup chopped white onion
- ½ cup halved green beans
- ½ cup snow peas
- 1 teaspoon minced garlic
- 2 teaspoons grated ginger, divided
- ½ tablespoon salt
- 1 tablespoon cornstarch
- 2 tablespoons soy sauce
- ¼ cup olive oil, divided
- 2 ½ tablespoons water

Directions:

- Take a large bowl, place 1 teaspoon grated ginger in it, add 2 tablespoons of olive oil, garlic, and cornstarch and then whisk well until cornstarch has dissolved.
- Add green beans, carrots, snow peas, and broccoli florets, and then toss until coated.
- Take a large skillet pan, place it over medium heat, add remaining oil and when hot, add vegetables and then cook for 2 minutes, tossing frequently.
- Add soy sauce and water into the pan along with onion and remaining ginger, season with salt, and then continue cooking for 3 to 4 minutes until vegetables turn tender-crisp.
- Serve straight away.

Nutritional Information per Serving:

Calories: 118.6 Cal; Fat: 9.3 g; Protein: 2.2 g; Carbs: 8 g; Fiber: 2.2 g;

DINNER RECIPES

Mushroom Sliders

Prep Time: 10 minutes; Cooking Time: 20 minutes; Yields: 4;

Ingredients:

- 4 Portobello mushrooms, destemmed
- 4 slider buns, small

For the Marinade:
- ¼ teaspoon dried thyme
- ½ tablespoon garlic powder
- ½ teaspoon salt
- ¼ cup balsamic vinegar
- ½ teaspoon dried basil
- 1 tablespoon Worcestershire
- ¼ teaspoon ground black pepper
- ¼ cup olive oil

Directions:

- Prepare the marinade and for this, take a small bowl, place all of its ingredients in it and then stir until well combined.

- Take a shallow dish, arrange the mushrooms in it, drizzle with the marinade until well coated, and then let them marinate for a minimum of 3 hours, flipping halfway.
- Take a griddle pan, place it over medium-high heat, grease with oil and then let it heat until hot.
- Place the marinated mushrooms on the grill pan and then cook for 5 to 10 minutes per side until thoroughly cooked and tender.
- When done, sandwich the mushrooms in the slider buns and then serve.

Nutritional Information per Serving:

Calories: 80 Cal; Fat: 3 g; Protein: 5 g; Carbs: 6 g; Fiber: 1 g;

Lentil and Turnip Soup

Prep Time: 10 minutes; Cooking Time: 25 minutes; Yields: 4;

Ingredients:

- 1 cup red lentils
- 2 medium white onions, peeled, sliced
- 14 ounces turnip, peeled, cubed
- 2 tablespoons lemon juice
- 2 ½ teaspoons salt
- 2 bay leaves
- 2 tablespoons lemon zest
- 4 tablespoons olive oil
- 6 cups boiling water

Directions:

- Take a large pot, place it over medium heat, add oil, and then let it heat.

- Add onions, cook for 5 minutes until onions turn tender, and then add turnip pieces along with red lentils and bay leaves.
- Pour in the water, stir until mixed, and then boil the soup for 15 minutes until lentils and turnip turn tender.
- Add salt, lemon juice, and zest into the juice, stir until mixed, and then cook for 3 minutes.
- Serve straight away.

Nutritional Information per Serving:

Calories: 111.7 Cal; Fat: 2 g; Protein: 6.7 g; Carbs: 18.2 g; Fiber: 6.4 g;

Tomato and Chickpea Curry

Prep Time: 5 minutes; Cooking Time: 15 minutes; Yields: 4;

Ingredients:

- 28 ounces cooked chickpeas
- 2 medium white onions, peeled, sliced
- 4 medium tomatoes, chopped
- 1 teaspoon salt
- 4 tablespoons olive oil
- 2 teaspoons curry powder
- 1 tablespoon soy sauce
- 1 teaspoon ground cumin
- 2 bay leaves
- 14 ounces coconut milk, unsweetened

Directions:

- Take a large pot, place it over medium-high heat, add oil and then let it heat until hot.
- Add onion, stir in salt and then cook for 2 minutes.
- Add bay leaves and all the spices, stir until mixed, and then cook for 1 minute.

- Add chickpeas, cook for another minute, add tomatoes and then continue cooking for 3 minutes.
- Add milk, simmer for 5 minutes until thoroughly hot, stir in soy sauce and then cook for 1 minute.
- Serve straight away.

Nutritional Information per Serving:

Calories: 177.3 Cal; Fat: 5 g; Protein: 6 g; Carbs: 29 g; Fiber: 6.2 g;

Lentil Stroganoff

Prep Time: 10 minutes; Cooking Time: 50 minutes; Yields: 4;

Ingredients:

- 1 cup brown lentils
- 1 medium white onion, peeled, chopped
- 2 dill pickles, cut into cubes
- 1 teaspoon salt
- ¼ teaspoon ground nutmeg
- 1 tablespoon paprika
- 1 tablespoon soy sauce
- 5 tablespoons tomato sauce
- 2 tablespoons cashew cream
- 3 cups of water

Directions:

- Take a medium pot, place it over medium-high heat, add lentil, and then pour in water.
- Add onion, stir until mixed, bring the mixture to a boil and then continue boiling the lentils for 40 minutes until lentils turn soft.
- Add pickles and tomato sauce, stir in salt, paprika, nutmeg, soy sauce, and cashew cream and bring the mixture to a boil.
- Serve straight away.

Nutritional Information per Serving:

Calories: 240 Cal; Fat: 100 g; Protein: 24.5 g; Carbs: 33 g; Fiber: 4 g;

Broccoli and Sun-dried Tomato Pasta

Prep Time: 10 minutes; Cooking Time: 20 minutes; Yields: 4;

Ingredients:

- 1 medium white onion, peeled, diced
- 3 cups broccoli florets
- 1 medium red bell pepper, cored, diced
- 4 ounces arugula
- 3 ounces sun-dried tomatoes, sliced
- 1 teaspoon salt
- ½ teaspoon ground black pepper
- 2 tablespoons olive oil
- 8 ounces whole-wheat pasta

For the Sauce:
- 3 cloves of garlic, peeled
- 1 cup cashews, roasted, unsalted
- 1 cup basil, fresh
- ½ of lemon, juiced
- ½ teaspoon salt
- 1 cup of water

Directions:

- Take a large pot half full with water, place it over medium-high heat and then bring it to a boil.
- Add pasta, cook for 8 minutes, then add broccoli florets and continue cooking for 2 minutes until pasta has turn tender and broccoli turn tender-crisp.
- Drain the pasta and broccoli florets, reserve 1 cup of cooking liquid, and then set aside until required.

- Prepare the sauce and for this, place all of its ingredients in a food processor and then pulse until smooth, set aside until required.
- Take a large skillet pan, place it over medium heat, add oil and let it heat until hot.
- Add onion and bell pepper, season with salt and black pepper, and cook for 5 minutes until vegetables turn tender.
- Add arugula and tomatoes, cook for 2 minutes until arugula leaves turn tender, and then add pasta and broccoli florets.
- Add the prepared sauce, toss until combined, stir in reserved cooking liquid and then cook for 2 minutes until thoroughly hot.
- Serve straight away.

Nutritional Information per Serving:

Calories: 312 Cal; Fat: 21 g; Protein: 7 g; Carbs: 27 g; Fiber: 6 g;

Creamy Broccoli Pasta

Prep Time: 5 minutes; Cooking Time: 25 minutes; Yields: 4;

Ingredients:

- 4 cups broccoli florets
- 16 ounces whole-wheat pasta
- 1 teaspoon onion powder
- 1 teaspoon garlic powder
- 6 tablespoons white whole-wheat flour
- 1 ½ teaspoon salt
- 4 tablespoons nutritional yeast
- ¾ teaspoon ground black pepper
- 4 tablespoons olive oil
- 2 ½ cups cashew milk, unsweetened

Directions:

- Take a large pot half full with water, place it over medium-high heat and then bring it to a boil.
- Add pasta, cook for 8 minutes, then add broccoli florets and continue cooking for 2 minutes until pasta has turn tender and broccoli turn tender-crisp.
- Drain the pasta and broccoli florets and then set aside until required.
- While pasta cooks, prepare the sauce, and for this, take a medium saucepan, place it over medium heat, add oil and then let it heat until hot.
- Whisk in flour until smooth, cook for 1 to 2 minutes until golden, and then gradually whisk in milk until smooth.
- Stir in salt, black pepper, onion powder, and garlic powder, switch heat to medium-low level and then continue cooking the sauce for 8 minutes until slightly thickened.
- Remove pan from heat, stir in the yeast until incorporated, and then taste the sauce to adjust seasoning.
- Add pasta and broccoli into the sauce, toss until coated, and then serve.

Nutritional Information per Serving:

Calories: 128 Cal; Fat: 10.3 g; Protein: 5.4 g; Carbs: 6.7 g; Fiber: 1.4 g;

Wild Rice Mushroom Soup

Prep Time: 5 minutes; Cooking Time: 40 minutes; Yields: 4;

Ingredients:

- ½ cup chopped white onion
- 8 ounces cremini mushrooms, sliced
- 1 jalapeño, chopped
- 1 tablespoon minced garlic

- 1 cup wild rice blend
- 1 teaspoon taco seasoning
- ½ teaspoon ground black pepper
- ¾ teaspoon salt
- ½ teaspoon red pepper flakes
- 1 teaspoon poultry seasoning
- ½ teaspoon dried thyme
- 2 teaspoons olive oil
- ½ cup cashew cream
- 4 cups of water
- ½ cup of salsa

Directions:

- Switch on the instant pot, press the sauté button, add oil into the inner pot and then let it heat.
- Add onion, mushrooms, jalapeno, and garlic, and then cook for 3 minutes until vegetable begin to soften.
- Add rice and salsa, stir in salt and all the spices and herbs until well mixed, press the cancel button, and then shut the instant pot with its lid.
- Press the manual button, cook at high pressure for 30 minutes, and when the instant pot beeps, do a natural pressure release.
- Stir the soup, add cashew cream, stir until well mixed, press the sauté button and then bring the soup to boil until thoroughly hot.
- Taste the soup to adjust seasoning and then serve.

Nutritional Information per Serving:

Calories: 274 Cal; Fat: 11 g; Protein: 10 g; Carbs: 38 g; Fiber: 5 g;

Kung Pao Lentils

Prep Time: 10 minutes; Cooking Time: 45 minutes; Yields: 3;

Ingredients:

For the Lentils:
- ½ cup brown lentils
- 1 ½ cups water
- ¼ teaspoon salt

For the Sauce:
- 3 tablespoons soy sauce
- 2 tablespoons of rice wine vinegar
- 1 tablespoon rice wine
- 1 teaspoon hoisin sauce
- 1 teaspoon toasted sesame oil
- 2 tablespoons maple syrup
- ¼ teaspoon lime zest
- 2 teaspoons cornstarch
- 3 tablespoons water

For the Vegetables:
- ¾ cup chopped celery
- 3 tablespoons cashews
- 1 medium green bell pepper, cored, chopped
- ½ cup chopped red onion
- 1 medium red bell pepper, cored, chopped
- 1 tablespoon minced garlic
- ½ teaspoon ground black pepper
- 1 teaspoon red pepper flakes
- 1-inch piece of ginger, grated
- 2 tablespoons lemon juice
- 2 teaspoon grapeseed oil

Directions:

- Prepare the lentils and for this, take a medium saucepan, place it over medium-high heat, add lentils in it, pour in water, and then stir in salt.
- Bring the lentils to boil, cook for 6 minutes, then switch heat to medium level, and then continue boiling for 25 minutes until lentils turn tender.
- When done, let the lentil rest for 5 minutes, drain excess liquid from the pan.
- Prepare the sauce and for this, take a medium bowl, place all of its ingredients in it and then stir until combined, set aside until required.
- Prepare the vegetables and for this, take a large skillet pan, place it over medium-high heat, add oil and then let it heat until hot.
- Add onion, cook for 3 minutes, add cashews and then cook for 1 minute.
- Stir in bell peppers, celery garlic, and ginger, cook for 4 minutes, add lentils, pour in the sauce, and then stir until mixed.
- Switch heat to the low level and then cook the lentils for 4 minutes until the sauce has thickened.
- Stir in red pepper flakes, black pepper, and lemon juice, and then serve.

Nutritional Information per Serving:

Calories: 283 Cal; Fat: 9 g; Protein: 12 g; Carbs: 37 g; Fiber: 12 g;

Orange Tofu

Prep Time: 10 minutes; Cooking Time: 35 minutes; Yields: 4;

Ingredients:

- 14 ounces tofu, firm, pressed, drained, cubed
- 1 teaspoon rice flour

- ¼ teaspoon garlic powder
- ¼ teaspoon salt
- 1/8 teaspoon ground black pepper
- 2 tablespoons cornstarch, divided
- 1 green onion, chopped

For the Sauce:
- 1/8 teaspoon salt
- 1 ½ tablespoons cornstarch
- 2 teaspoons minced garlic
- 1 tablespoon grated ginger
- 2 tablespoons soy sauce
- 3 tablespoons maple syrup
- 1 teaspoon Sriracha sauce
- 2 tablespoons white vinegar
- 1 cup of orange juice
- ¼ cup vegetable broth

Directions:

- Switch on the oven, then set it to 400 degrees F and let it preheat.
- Take a large bowl, place tofu pieces in it, sprinkle with salt, black pepper, garlic powder, flour, and 1 tablespoon cornstarch, and then toss until coated.
- Sprinkle remaining cornstarch over the tofu pieces, toss until coated, and then set aside until required.
- Take a baking dish, spread tofu pieces in it and then bake for 35 minutes until nicely golden brown on all sides, tossing halfway.
- Prepare the sauce and for this, take a small saucepan, place it over medium heat, and then add all of its ingredients in it except for cornstarch and water.
- Whisk until combined, bring the sauce to a boil, whisk together cornstarch and water, whisk into the sauce until

- combined, and then simmer the sauce for 2 minutes or until thickened to the desired level.
- When tofu has baked, pour the sauce over the tofu and then toss until coated.
- Garnish green onion over the tofu and then serve.

Nutritional Information per Serving:

Calories: 193 Cal; Fat: 4 g; Protein: 10 g; Carbs: 27 g; Fiber: 1 g;

Lentil Brown Rice Soup

Prep Time: 10 minutes; Cooking Time: 50 minutes; Yields: 4;

Ingredients:

- ½ cup diced carrots
- ½ cup brown lentils, soaked
- 1 cup broccoli florets
- 1/3 cup brown rice, soaked
- ½ cup diced red bell pepper
- ½ of a medium white onion, peeled, chopped
- 1 cup baby spinach
- 1 ½ cups diced tomatoes
- 1 green chili, chopped
- 1 tablespoon minced garlic
- 1-inch piece of ginger, grated
- ¾ teaspoon salt
- ½ teaspoon turmeric powder
- ¼ teaspoon ground black pepper
- ½ teaspoon cumin seeds
- 1 bay leaf
- ½ teaspoon mustard seeds
- ½ teaspoon paprika
- 1 teaspoon coriander powder

- ½ teaspoon curry powder
- ¼ teaspoon chipotle pepper
- 1 teaspoon lemon juice
- 1 tablespoon olive oil
- 2 teaspoons ketchup
- 4 cups of water

Directions:

- Take a large saucepan, place it over medium heat, add oil and then let it heat until hot.
- Add mustard and cumin seeds, cook for 1 minute until golden, add onion, ginger, garlic, and bay leaf, and then continue cooking for 5 minutes.
- Add all the spices, stir until mixed, cook for 1 minute, add tomatoes, and then cook for 5 minutes until mixture turn saucy.
- Add all the vegetables, season with salt, add ketchup and then stir until mixed.
- Add rice and lentils, pour in the water, stir until mixed, cover the pan with its lid and then cook for 40 minutes until lentils and vegetables have thoroughly cooked.
- When done, add spinach into the soup, stir until mixed, and then continue cooking for 5 minutes until spinach leaves wilt.
- Serve straight away.

Nutritional Information per Serving:

Calories: 205 Cal; Fat: 2 g; Protein: 9.5 g; Carbs: 37 g; Fiber: 10 g;

Peanut and Lentil Soup

Prep Time: 5 minutes; Cooking Time: 35 minutes; Yields: 3;

Ingredients:

- ½ cup red lentils

- ½ cup diced zucchini
- ½ cup diced sweet potato
- ½ cup diced potato
- ½ cup chopped broccoli florets
- ½ of a medium onion, peeled, chopped
- 2 tomatoes
- ½ cup baby spinach
- 2 tablespoons peanuts
- 4 cloves of garlic, peeled
- 1-inch piece of ginger
- 1 ½ teaspoon ground cumin
- ¾ teaspoon salt
- ¼ teaspoon ground black pepper
- 2 teaspoons ground coriander
- 1 ½ teaspoon Harissa Spice Blend
- 1 tablespoon sambal oelek
- 1 teaspoon lemon juice
- ¼ cup peanut butter
- 1 tablespoon tomato paste
- 1 teaspoon olive oil
- 2 ½ cups vegetable stock
- 2 tablespoons chopped cilantro

Directions:

- Take a large saucepan, place it over medium heat, add oil and then let it heat.
- Add onion, stir until coated in oil, and then cook for 5 minutes.
- Place tomatoes in a blender, add garlic, ginger, all the spices, tomato paste, and chili sauce, and then pulse until pureed.
- Pour the tomato mixture into the onion mixture, stir until mixed, and then cook for 5 minutes.
- Add half of the nuts, lentils, and all the vegetables, stir in salt, peanut butter, and lemon juice, pour in the stock, cover the

pan with its lid and then cook for 20 minutes until vegetables turn tender.
- Add spinach, continue cooking for 5 minutes, garnish with cilantro, and then serve.

Nutritional Information per Serving:

Calories: 411 Cal; Fat: 17 g; Protein: 20 g; Carbs: 50 g; Fiber: 18 g;

Lentil with Spinach

Prep Time: 5 minutes; Cooking Time: 25 minutes; Yields: 2;

Ingredients:

- ½ cup red lentils
- 1 cup chopped spinach
- ½ teaspoon mustard seeds
- ½ teaspoon ground turmeric
- 1/3 teaspoon cumin seeds
- 1/3 teaspoon cayenne
- 1/3 teaspoon nigella seeds
- 2/3 teaspoon salt
- 1/8 teaspoon fennel seeds
- 1/8 teaspoon fenugreek seeds
- 1 teaspoon olive oil
- 2 ½ cups water

Directions:

- Take a large saucepan, place it over medium heat, add oil and then let it heat until hot.
- Add all the seeds, stir until coated in oil, and then cook for 1 to 2 minutes until seeds begin to pop.

- Stir in cayenne pepper and turmeric, stir in lentils and then cook for 1 minute until roasted.
- Season with salt, pour in the water, and then cook for 20 minutes until lentils have thoroughly cooked; cover the pan partially with its lid.
- Stir in spinach, simmer for 2 minutes until spinach leaves wilts, and then serve.

Nutritional Information per Serving:

Calories: 193 Cal; Fat: 3 g; Protein: 12 g; Carbs: 28 g; Fiber: 14 g;

Lentil Loaf

Prep Time: 10 minutes; Cooking Time: 45 minutes; Yields: 8;

Ingredients:

For the Loaf:
- 1 cup chopped onion
- 1 cup quick-cooking oats
- ½ cup chopped carrot
- 1 ½ cups cooked lentils
- ½ cup chopped celery
- 2 tablespoons ground flax seeds
- 1 teaspoon minced garlic
- ½ teaspoon of sea salt
- 1/8 teaspoon cayenne pepper
- 1/8 teaspoon ground black pepper
- 1 teaspoon dried thyme
- ½ cup chopped walnuts
- 2 tablespoons soy sauce
- 1 tablespoon olive oil

For the Glaze:

- 1/8 teaspoon salt
- 2 tablespoons maple syrup
- 2 tablespoons tomato paste
- 1 tablespoon apple cider vinegar

Directions:

- Switch on the oven, then set it to 375 degrees F and let it preheat.
- Take a 9-by-5 inch loaf pan, line it with parchment paper, and then set aside until required.
- Take a large skillet pan, place it over medium heat, add oil and then let it heat.
- Add carrot, onion, and celery, stir in garlic and then cook for 10 minutes until vegetables turn softened.
- When done, spoon the vegetables into the blender, add lentils, nuts, oats, flaxseeds, salt, cayenne pepper, black pepper, soy sauce, and then pulse until well combined.
- Spoon the mixture into the prepared loaf pan, and then press it firmly.
- Prepare the glaze and for this, take a small bowl, place all of its ingredients in it, whisk until combined, and then spread this mixture on top of the loaf.
- Place the loaf pan into the oven and then bake for 30 minutes until the loaf has thoroughly cooked.
- When done, let the loaf cool for 10 minutes, lift it out with the parchment sheet, and then cut it into slices.
- Serve straight away.

Nutritional Information per Serving:

Calories: 166 Cal; Fat: 8 g; Protein: 6 g; Carbs: 19 g; Fiber: 5 g;

Chorizo

Prep Time: 5 minutes; Cooking Time: 40 minutes; Yields: 4;

Ingredients:

- 28 ounces tofu, firm, pressed, drained, crumbled
- 1 small white onion, peeled, chopped
- 1 tablespoon minced garlic
- 1 teaspoon salt
- 1 tablespoon red chili powder
- ½ teaspoon ground black pepper
- ⅛ teaspoon ground cinnamon
- 1 teaspoon ground cumin
- 1 teaspoon apple cider vinegar
- 2 tablespoons olive oil
- 2 tablespoons chopped cilantro

Directions:

- Take a large skillet pan, place it over medium-high heat, add oil and then let it heat.
- Add onion and garlic, stir until coated with oil, season with salt and black pepper, and then cook for 5 minutes until vegetables turn soft.
- Add tofu, stir until well mixed and then cook for 15 to 30 minutes until tofu turns nicely brown and crisp.
- Stir in red chili powder, cinnamon, and cumin, cook for 1 to 2 minutes until fragrant, stir in vinegar, and then taste to adjust seasoning.
- When done, garnish tofu with cilantro and then serve.

Nutritional Information per Serving:

Calories: 314 Cal; Fat: 21 g; Protein: 26 g; Carbs: 11 g; Fiber: 5 g;

Spiced Carrot and Millet Salad

Prep Time: 10 minutes; Cooking Time: 20 minutes; Yields: 3;

Ingredients:

- 2 medium carrots, peeled, thin angle slices
- ¾ cup millet
- 2 cups cooked chickpeas
- 1 large red onion, peeled, sliced
- 1 ½ teaspoon garlic powder
- 1/3 cup sultanas
- ½ cup chopped walnuts
- 1 teaspoon salt
- 1 teaspoon turmeric powder
- ½ teaspoon paprika powder
- ¼ cup olive oil
- 2 tablespoons chopped coriander
- 1 ½ cup water

Directions:

- Switch on the oven, then set it to 200 degrees F and let it preheat.
- Meanwhile, take a large bowl, place onion and carrots in it, sprinkle with garlic, salt, turmeric, and paprika, drizzle with oil, and then toss until coated.
- Take a baking tray, line it with a parchment sheet, spread vegetables in it, and then bake for 20 minutes or more until roasted, turning halfway.
- Meanwhile, prepare the millet, and for this, take a medium saucepan, place it over medium-high heat, and then pour in water.
- Bring the water to a boil, add millet and then simmer for 10 minutes until millet absorbed all of the cooking liquid, covering the pan with the lid.

- When done, remove the pan from heat, let the millet rest for 5 minutes and then stir it.
- When vegetables have roasted, transfer them into a large bowl, add millet and remaining ingredients and then toss until mixed.
- Serve straight away.

Nutritional Information per Serving:

Calories: 434 Cal; Fat: 32 g; Protein: 6 g; Carbs: 36 g; Fiber: 5 g;

Carrots and Quinoa Veggie Bowl

Prep Time: 10 minutes; Cooking Time: 0 minutes; Yields: 3;

Ingredients:

- 2/3 cup quinoa
- 7 kale leaves, de-stemmed, chopped
- 2 cups cooked chickpeas
- 2 carrots, spiralized
- ½ of an orange, peeled, sliced
- 2 green onions, sliced
- 1 large avocado, peeled, pitted, sliced
- 1 cup chopped parsley
- ½ teaspoon salt
- ½ teaspoon ground black pepper
- 2 tablespoons toasted walnuts, crushed
- ½ of a lemon, juiced

Directions:

- Prepare the quinoa, and for this, cook by following the instruction on its package and, when done, fluff it with a fork and set aside until required.

- Meanwhile, place chopped kale leaves in a large, drizzle with lemon juice, sprinkle with some salt and black pepper, and then massage for 1 minute.
- Scatter kale leaves evenly among three plates, top with chickpeas, quinoa, carrots, and parsley, season with salt and black pepper, and then drizzle with lemon juice.
- Scatter orange and avocado slices evenly on top of the salad, sprinkle with walnuts and then serve.

Nutritional Information per Serving:

Calories: 506 Cal; Fat: 21 g; Protein: 21 g; Carbs: 68 g; Fiber: 23 g;

Pasta Primavera

Prep Time: 5 minutes; Cooking Time: 10 minutes; Yields: 2;

Ingredients:

- 8 ounces whole-wheat spaghetti
- 2 portabella mushrooms, sliced
- 1/2 pound asparagus, chopped
- 2 cups broccoli florets, chopped
- 3 cups chopped spinach leaves
- 2 teaspoons minced garlic
- 2 cups frozen peas
- 1 ½ teaspoon salt
- ½ teaspoon onion powder
- 1 teaspoon Dijon mustard
- 2 teaspoons dried oregano
- 1 tablespoon soy sauce
- 2 tablespoons lemon juice
- 6 tablespoons olive oil, divided

Directions:

- Prepare the pasta, and for this, take a large pot half full with water, place it over medium-high heat and then bring it to a boil.
- Add pasta, and then cook for 10 to 12 minutes until pasta has turn tender.
- When pasta has cooked, drain it, transfer in a bowl, add 2 tablespoons of oil and then toss until coated, set aside until required.
- Cook the vegetables, and for this, take a large skillet pan, place it over medium-high heat, add 2 tablespoons of oil and then let it heat.
- Add mushrooms, cook for 2 minutes, stir in soy sauce and then continue cooking for 1 minute.
- Add asparagus and broccoli, cook for 3 minutes, add spinach and then continue cooking for 1 minute until spinach leaves wilt.
- Add peas, cook for 1 minute, stir in garlic and then continue cooking for 1 minute until fragrant.
- Take a small bowl, place remaining oil in it, add oregano, onion powder, lemon juice, and mustard and then stir until combined.
- When vegetables have cooked, add pasta into the pan, drizzle with the oil-spice mixture, toss until combined, and then stir in salt until mixed.
- Serve straight away.

Nutritional Information per Serving:

Calories: 421 Cal; Fat: 15.7 g; Protein: 14.4 g; Carbs: 58.4 g; Fiber: 7.5 g;

Chickpea Burgers

Prep Time: 10 minutes; Cooking Time: 30 minutes; Yields: 4;

Ingredients:

For the Burgers:
- ½ of a medium red onion, peeled, grated
- 1 ½ cup cooked chickpeas
- 1 large carrot, grated
- 1 teaspoon minced garlic
- ¼ cup white whole-wheat flour
- 1 teaspoon salt
- ½ teaspoon ground black pepper
- 1 teaspoon ground cumin
- 2 teaspoons smoked paprika
- ¼ cup olive oil
- 2 tablespoons tahini

For Serving:
- 4 whole-wheat burger buns
- 4 tablespoons BBQ sauce
- 4 leaves of lettuce
- 4 slices of tomato
- 4 slices of red onion

Directions:

- Switch on the oven, then set it to 400 degrees F and let it preheat.
- Meanwhile, take a large bowl, place chickpeas in it, and then mash with a fork.
- Add carrot, onion, and garlic, stir until mixed and then stir in flour, all the spices, and tahini until well combined and then shape the mixture into four patties.
- Take a large skillet pan, place it over medium-high heat, add oil and then let it heat until hot.
- Add prepared patties in it and then cook for 3 to 4 minutes per side until golden brown.
- Transfer the patties to a baking sheet lined with parchment paper and then bake for 20 minutes until thoroughly cooked and nicely browned, turning patties halfway.

- Assemble the burger and for this, layer the bottom half of the burger bun with a lettuce leaf and then place a patty on it.
- Top with a slice of tomato and onion, drizzle with 1 tablespoon of BBQ sauce, and then cover with the top half of the bun.
- Serve straight away.

Nutritional Information per Serving:

Calories: 298 Cal; Fat: 19.8 g; Protein: 7.4 g; Carbs: 26 g; Fiber: 6.2 g;

Wild Rice Soup

Prep Time: 10 minutes; Cooking Time: 55 minutes; Yields: 8;

Ingredients:

- 1 cup northern white beans, uncooked
- 1 cup wild rice
- 1 medium white onion, peeled, diced
- 4 medium carrots, peeled, sliced
- 2 celery ribs, sliced
- 8 ounces baby Bella mushrooms, sliced
- ½ cup roasted cashews
- 2 tablespoons minced garlic
- 2 ½ teaspoons salt, divided
- 1 tablespoon dried thyme
- ½ teaspoon ground black pepper
- 2 tablespoons dried oregano
- 2 teaspoons dried sage
- 1 tablespoon soy sauce
- 2 tablespoons olive oil
- 8 cups vegetable broth

Directions:

- Take a medium bowl, place cashews in it, cover with hot water, and then let them soak until required.
- Plugin the instant pot, add oil into the inner pot, press the saute button, and then let it heat.
- Add onion, carrot, and celery, cook for 5 minutes until vegetables turn golden brown, add mushrooms and then cook for 2 minutes.
- Stir in thyme, oregano, and garlic, cook for 2 minutes, add rice and beans, and then pour in broth.
- Stir in 2 teaspoons salt and black pepper, cover the instant pot with its lid, press the manual button, and then cook for 45 minutes at a high-pressure setting.
- When the instant pot beeps, do a quick pressure release, open the instant pot, remove 2 cups of the soup and pour into a blender.
- Drain the cashews, add them into the blender along with sage and then blend for 1 minute until creamy.
- Pour the soup into the instant pot, stir in remaining salt and soy sauce until well combined, and then serve.

Nutritional Information per Serving:

Calories: 247 Cal; Fat: 9.7 g; Protein: 8.7 g; Carbs: 34.2 g; Fiber: 5.7 g;

Sesame Cauliflower

Prep Time: 10 minutes; Cooking Time: 20 minutes; Yields: 4;

Ingredients:

- 6 ½ cups chopped cauliflower florets
- 1 ½ tablespoon cornstarch
- ¼ cup of water
- 2 teaspoons sesame seeds
- 1 scallion, chopped

For the Sauce:

- 1 tablespoon minced garlic
- ½ teaspoon ginger powder
- ¼ cup maple syrup
- 1/3 cup soy sauce
- ¼ cup of rice vinegar
- 1 ½ teaspoon sesame oil

Directions:

- Switch on the oven, then set it to 450 degrees F and let it preheat.
- Meanwhile, take a large baking sheet, grease it with oil, and then spread cauliflower florets on it in a single layer.
- Place the baking sheet into the oven and then bake for 20 minutes until the florets turn golden brown, turning halfway.
- Meanwhile, take a small saucepan, add all the ingredients for the sauce in it and then whisk until combined.
- Place the sauce over medium heat, bring it to boil, and then cook for 2 minutes or until thickened slightly.
- When florets have roasted, pour the sauce over them and then toss until coated.
- Sprinkle scallion and sesame seeds over the cauliflower florets and then serve.

Nutritional Information per Serving:

Calories: 449 Cal; Fat: 9 g; Protein: 16 g; Carbs: 78 g; Fiber: 8 g;

Potato Curry

Prep Time: 10 minutes; Cooking Time: 35 minutes; Yields: 6;

Ingredients:

- 15 ounces cooked chickpeas

- 4 potatoes, peeled, cubed
- 15 ounces cooked peas
- 14.5 ounces diced tomatoes
- 1 large white onion, peeled, diced
- 1-inch piece of ginger root, peeled, grated
- 1 tablespoon minced garlic
- 2 teaspoons salt
- 1 ½ teaspoons cayenne pepper
- 4 teaspoons curry powder
- 2 teaspoons ground cumin
- 4 teaspoons garam masala
- 2 tablespoons olive oil
- 14 ounces coconut milk, unsweetened

Directions:

- Take a large pot, place potato cubes in it, cover with salty water, and then place it over high heat.
- Bring the potatoes to boil, switch heat to medium-low level, cover the pot with its lid and then simmer potatoes for 15 minutes until tender.
- When done, drain the potatoes and then set aside until required.
- Then take a large skillet pan, place it over medium heat, add oil and then let it heat until hot.
- Add onion and garlic, cook for 5 minutes until onion turned tender, stir all the seasonings and spices, and then cook for another 2 minutes.
- Add peas, chickpeas, tomatoes, and boiled potatoes, pour in the coconut milk, stir until mixed, and then bring the curry to simmer.
- Continue cooking the curry for 5 to 10 minutes until thickened to the desired level, and then serve.

Nutritional Information per Serving:

Calories: 407 Cal; Fat: 20.1 g; Protein: 10.1 g; Carbs: 50.6 g; Fiber: 10.1 g;

DESSERT RECIPES

Raspberry Muffins

Prep Time: 10 minutes; Cooking Time: 25 minutes; Yields: 12;

Ingredients:

- ½ cup and 2 tablespoons whole-wheat flour
- 1 ½ cup raspberries, fresh and more for decorating
- 1 cup white whole-wheat flour
- 1/8 teaspoon salt
- ¾ cup of coconut sugar
- 2 teaspoons baking powder
- 1 teaspoon apple cider vinegar
- 1 ¼ cups water
- ½ cup olive oil

Directions:

- Switch on the oven, then set it to 400 degrees F and let it preheat.
- Meanwhile, take a large bowl, place both flours in it, add salt and baking powder and then stir until combined.
- Take a medium bowl, add oil to it, and then whisk in the sugar until dissolved.

- Whisk in vinegar and water until blended, slowly stir in flour mixture until smooth batter comes together, and then fold in berries.
- Take a 12-cups muffin pan, grease it with oil, fill evenly with the prepared mixture and then put a raspberry on top of each muffin.
- Bake the muffins for 25 minutes until the top golden brown, and then serve.

Nutritional Information per Serving:

Calories: 109 Cal; Fat: 3.4 g; Protein: 2.1 g; Carbs: 17.6 g; Fiber: 1 g;

Chocolate Chip Cake

Prep Time: 10 minutes; Cooking Time: 50 minutes; Yields: 10;

Ingredients:

- 2 cups white whole-wheat flour
- ¼ teaspoon baking soda
- 1/3 cup coconut sugar
- 2 teaspoons baking powder
- ½ teaspoon salt
- ½ cup chocolate chips, vegan
- 1 teaspoon vanilla extract, unsweetened
- 1 tablespoon applesauce
- 1 teaspoon apple cider vinegar
- ¼ cup melted coconut oil
- ½ teaspoon almond extract, unsweetened
- 1 cup almond milk, unsweetened

Directions:

- Switch on the oven, then set it to 360 degrees F and let it preheat.
- Meanwhile, take a 9-by-5 inches loaf pan, grease it with oil, and then set aside until required.
- Take a large bowl, add sugar to it, pour in oil, vanilla and almond extract, vinegar, and milk, and then whisk until well combined.
- Take a large bowl, place flour in it, add salt, baking powder, and soda, and then stir until mixed.
- Stir the flour mixture into the milk mixture until smooth batter comes together, and then fold in 1/3 cup of chocolate chips.
- Spoon the batter into the loaf pan, scatter remaining chocolate chips on top and then bake for 50 minutes.
- When done, let the bread cool for 10 minutes and then cut it into slices.
- Serve straight away.

Nutritional Information per Serving:

Calories: 218 Cal; Fat: 8 g; Protein: 3.4 g; Carbs: 32 g; Fiber: 2 g;

Coffee Cake

Prep Time: 10 minutes; Cooking Time: 45 minutes; Yields: 9;

Ingredients:

For the Cake:
- 1/3 cup coconut sugar
- 1 tablespoon coffee
- 1 teaspoon vanilla extract, unsweetened
- ¼ cup olive oil
- 1/8 teaspoon almond extract, unsweetened
- 1 ¾ cup white whole-wheat flour
- 2 teaspoons baking powder

- ½ teaspoon salt
- ¼ teaspoon baking soda
- 1 teaspoon apple cider vinegar
- 1 tablespoon applesauce
- 1 cup almond milk, unsweetened

For the Streusel:
- ½ cup white whole-wheat flour
- 2 teaspoons cinnamon
- 1/3 cup coconut sugar
- ½ teaspoon salt
- 2 tablespoons olive oil
- 1 tablespoon coconut butter

Directions:

- Switch on the oven, then set it to 350 degrees F and let it preheat.
- Meanwhile, take a large bowl, pour in milk, add applesauce, vinegar, sugar, oil, vanilla, coffee, and almond extract and then whisk until blended.
- Take a medium bowl, place flour in it, add salt, baking powder, and soda and then stir until mixed.
- Stir the flour mixture into the milk mixture until smooth batter comes together, and then spoon the mixture into a loaf pan lined with parchment paper.
- Prepare streusel and for this, take a medium bowl, place flour in it, and then add sugar, salt, and cinnamon.
- Stir until mixed, and then mix butter and oil with fingers until the crumble mixture comes together.
- Spread the prepared streusel on top of the batter of the cake and then bake for 45 minutes until the top turn golden brown and cake have thoroughly cooked.
- When done, let the cake rest in its pan for 10 minutes, remove it to cool completely and then cut it into slices.
- Serve straight away.

Nutritional Information per Serving:

Calories: 259 Cal; Fat: 10 g; Protein: 3 g; Carbs: 37 g; Fiber: 1 g;

Chocolate Marble Cake

Prep Time: 15 minutes; Cooking Time: 50 minutes; Yields: 8;

Ingredients:

- 1 ½ cup white whole-wheat flour
- 1 tablespoon flaxseed meal
- 2 ½ tablespoons cocoa powder
- ¼ teaspoon salt
- 4 tablespoons chopped walnuts
- 1 teaspoon baking powder
- 2/3 cup coconut sugar
- ¼ teaspoon baking soda
- 1 teaspoon vanilla extract, unsweetened
- 3 tablespoons peanut butter
- ¼ cup olive oil
- 1 cup almond milk, unsweetened

Directions:

- Switch on the oven, then set it to 350 degrees F and let it preheat.
- Meanwhile, take a medium bowl, place flour in it, add salt, baking powder, and soda in it and then stir until mixed.
- Take a large bowl, pour in milk, add sugar, flaxseed, oil, and vanilla, whisk until sugar has dissolved, and then whisk in flour mixture until smooth batter comes together.
- Spoon half of the prepared batter in a medium bowl, add cocoa powder and then stir until combined.

- Add peanut butter into the other bowl and then stir until combined.
- Take a loaf pan, line it with a parchment sheet, spoon half of the chocolate batter in it, and then spread it evenly.
- Layer half of the chocolate batter with half of the peanut butter batter, cover with the remaining chocolate batter and then layer with the remaining peanut butter batter.
- Make swirls into the batter with a toothpick, smooth the top with a spatula, sprinkle walnuts on top, and then bake for 50 minutes until done.
- When done, let the cake rest in its pan for 10 minutes, then remove it to cool completely and cut it into slices.
- Serve straight away.

Nutritional Information per Serving:

Calories: 299 Cal; Fat: 14 g; Protein: 6 g; Carbs: 39 g; Fiber: 3 g;

Chocolate Chip Cookies

Prep Time: 10 minutes; Cooking Time: 10 minutes; Yields: 22;

Ingredients:

- 1 ¼ cups white whole-wheat flour
- 1 ½ tablespoon flax seeds
- ½ teaspoon baking soda
- ½ cup of coconut sugar
- ¼ teaspoon of sea salt
- ¼ cup powdered coconut sugar
- 1 teaspoon baking powder
- 2 teaspoons vanilla extract, unsweetened
- 4 ½ tablespoons water
- ½ cup of coconut oil
- 1 cup chocolate chips, vegan

Directions:

- Take a large bowl, place flax seeds in it, stir in water and then let the mixture rest for 5 minutes until creamy.
- Then add remaining ingredients into the flax seeds mixture except for flour and chocolate chips and then beat until light batter comes together.
- Beat in flour, ¼ cup at a time, until smooth batter comes together, and then fold in chocolate chips.
- Use an ice cream scoop to scoop the batter onto a baking sheet lined with parchment sheet with some distance between cookies and then bake for 10 minutes until cookies turn golden brown.
- When done, let the cookies cool on the baking sheet for 3 minutes and then cool completely on the wire rack for 5 minutes.
- Serve straight away.

Nutritional Information per Serving:

Calories: 141 Cal; Fat: 7 g; Protein: 1 g; Carbs: 17 g; Fiber: 2 g;

Lemon Cake

Prep Time: 10 minutes; Cooking Time: 50 minutes; Yields: 9;

Ingredients:

- 1 ½ cup white whole-wheat flour
- 1 ½ teaspoon baking powder
- 2 tablespoons almond flour
- 1 lemon zest
- ¼ teaspoon baking soda
- 1/8 teaspoon turmeric powder
- 1/3 teaspoon salt

- ¼ teaspoon vanilla extract, unsweetened
- 1/3 cup lemon juice
- ½ cup maple syrup
- ¼ cup olive oil
- ¼ cup of water

For the Frosting:
- 1 tablespoon lemon juice
- 1/8 teaspoon salt
- ¼ cup maple syrup
- 2 tablespoons powdered sugar
- 6 ounces vegan cream cheese, softened

Directions:

- Switch on the oven, then set it to 350 degrees F and let it preheat.
- Take a large bowl, pour in water, lemon juice, and oil, add vanilla extract and maple syrup, and whisk until blended.
- Whisk in flour, ¼ cup at a time, until smooth, and then whisk in almond flour, salt, turmeric, lemon zest, baking soda, and powder until well combined.
- Take a loaf pan, grease it with oil, spoon prepared batter in it, and then bake for 50 minutes.
- Meanwhile, prepare the frosting and for this, take a small bowl, place all of its ingredients in it, whisk until smooth, and then let it chill until required.
- When the cake has cooked, let it cool for 10 minutes in its pan and then let it cool completely on the wire rack.
- Spread the prepared frosting on top of the cake, slice the cake, and then serve.

Nutritional Information per Serving:

Calories: 275 Cal; Fat: 12 g; Protein: 3 g; Carbs: 38 g; Fiber: 1 g;

Banana Muffins

Prep Time: 10 minutes; Cooking Time: 30 minutes; Yields: 12;

Ingredients:

- 1 ½ cups mashed banana
- 1 ½ cups and 2 tablespoons white whole-wheat flour, divided
- ¼ cup of coconut sugar
- ¾ cup rolled oats, divided
- 1 teaspoon ginger powder
- 1 tablespoon ground cinnamon, divided
- 2 teaspoons baking powder
- ½ teaspoon salt
- 1 teaspoon baking soda
- 1 tablespoon vanilla extract, unsweetened
- ½ cup maple syrup
- 1 tablespoon rum
- ½ cup of coconut oil

Directions:

- Switch on the oven, then set it to 350 degrees F and let it preheat.
- Meanwhile, take a medium bowl, place 1 ½ cup flour in it, add ½ cup oats, ginger, baking powder and soda, salt, and 2 teaspoons cinnamon and then stir until mixed.
- Place ¼ cup of coconut oil in a heatproof bowl, melt it in the microwave oven and then whisk in maple syrup until combined.
- Add mashed banana along with rum and vanilla, stir until combined, and then whisk this mixture into the flour mixture until smooth batter comes together.
- Take a separate medium bowl, place remaining oats and flour in it, add cinnamon, coconut sugar, and coconut oil and then stir with a fork until crumbly mixture comes together.

- Take a 12-cups muffin pan, fill evenly with prepared batter, top with oats mixture, and then bake for 30 minutes until firm and the top turn golden brown.
- When done, let the muffins cool for 5 minutes in its pan and then cool the muffins completely before serving.

Nutritional Information per Serving:

Calories: 240 Cal; Fat: 9.3 g; Protein: 2.6 g; Carbs: 35.4 g; Fiber: 2 g;

No-Bake Cookies

Prep Time: 30 minutes; Cooking Time: 0 minutes; Yields: 9;

Ingredients:

- 1 cup rolled oats
- ¼ cup of cocoa powder
- 1/8 teaspoon salt
- 1 teaspoon vanilla extract, unsweetened
- ¼ cup and 2 tablespoons peanut butter, divided
- 6 tablespoons coconut oil, divided
- ¼ cup and 1 tablespoon maple syrup, divided

Directions:

- Take a small saucepan, place it over low heat, add 5 tablespoons of coconut oil and then let it melt.
- Whisk in 2 tablespoons peanut butter, salt, 1 teaspoon vanilla extract, and ¼ cup each of cocoa powder and maple syrup, and then whisk until well combined.
- Remove pan from heat, stir in oats and then spoon the mixture evenly into 9 cups of a muffin pan.
- Wipe clean the pan, return it over low heat, add remaining coconut oil, maple syrup, and peanut butter, stir until

combined, and then cook for 2 minutes until thoroughly warmed.
- Drizzle the peanut butter sauce over the oat mixture in the muffin pan and then let it freeze for 20 minutes or more until set.
- Serve straight away.

Nutritional Information per Serving:

Calories: 213 Cal; Fat: 14.8 g; Protein: 4 g; Carbs: 17.3 g; Fiber: 2.1 g;

Peanut Butter and Oat Bars

Prep Time: 40 minutes; Cooking Time: 8 minutes; Yields: 8;

Ingredients:

- 1 cup rolled oats
- 1/8 teaspoon salt
- ¼ cup chocolate chips, vegan
- ¼ cup maple syrup
- 1 cup peanut butter

Directions:

- Take a medium saucepan, place it over medium heat, add peanut butter, salt, and maple syrup and then whisk until combined and thickened; this will take 5 minutes.
- Remove pan from heat, place oats in a bowl, pour peanut butter mixture on it and then stir until well combined.
- Take an 8-by-6 inches baking dish, line it with a parchment sheet, spoon the oats mixture in it, and then spread evenly, pressing the mixture into the dish.
- Sprinkle the chocolate chips on top, press them into the bar mixture and then let the mixture rest in the refrigerator for 30 minutes or more until set.

- When ready to eat, cut the bar mixture into even size pieces and then serve.

Nutritional Information per Serving:

Calories: 274 Cal; Fat: 17 g; Protein: 10 g; Carbs: 19 g; Fiber: 3 g;

Baked Apples

Prep Time: 5 minutes; Cooking Time: 20 minutes; Yields: 4;

Ingredients:

- 6 medium apples, peeled, cut into chunks
- 1 teaspoon ground cinnamon
- 2 tablespoons melted coconut oil

Directions:

- Switch on the oven, then set it to 350 degrees F and let it preheat.
- Take a medium baking dish, and then spread apple pieces in it.
- Take a small bowl, place coconut oil in it, stir in cinnamon, drizzle this mixture over apples and then toss until coated.
- Place the baking dish into the oven and then bake for 20 minutes or more until apples turn soft, stirring halfway.
- Serve straight away.

Nutritional Information per Serving:

Calories: 170 Cal; Fat: 3.8 g; Protein: 0.5 g; Carbs: 31 g; Fiber: 5.5 g;

Chocolate Strawberry Shake

Prep Time: 5 minutes; Cooking Time: 0 minutes; Yields: 2;

Ingredients:

- 2 cups almond milk, unsweetened
- 4 bananas, peeled, frozen
- 4 tablespoons cocoa powder
- 2 cups strawberries, frozen

Directions:

- Place all the ingredients into the jar of a high-speed food processor or blender in the order stated in the ingredients list and then cover it with the lid.
- Pulse for 1 minute until smooth, and then serve.

Nutritional Information per Serving:

Calories: 208 Cal; Fat: 0.2 g; Protein: 12.4 g; Carbs: 26.2 g; Fiber: 1.4 g;

Chocolate Clusters

Prep Time: 15 minutes; Cooking Time: 0 minutes; Yields: 24;

Ingredients:

- 1 cup chopped dark chocolate, vegan
- 1 cup cashews, roasted, salt
- 1 teaspoon sea salt flakes

Directions:

- Take a large baking sheet, line it with wax paper, and then set aside until required.

- Take a medium bowl, place chocolate in it, and then microwave for 1 minute.
- Stir the chocolate and then continue microwaving it at 1-minute intervals until chocolate melts completely, stirring at every interval.
- When melted, stir the chocolate to bring it to 90 degrees F and then stir in cashews.
- Scoop the walnut-chocolate mixture on the prepared baking sheet, ½ tablespoons per cluster, and then sprinkle with salt.
- Let the clusters stand at room temperature until harden and then serve.

Nutritional Information per Serving:

Calories: 79.4 Cal; Fat: 6.6 g; Protein: 1 g; Carbs: 5.8 g; Fiber: 1.1 g;

Banana Coconut Cookies

Prep Time: 40 minutes; Cooking Time: 0 minutes; Yields: 8;

Ingredients:

- 1 ½ cup shredded coconut, unsweetened
- 1 cup mashed banana

Directions:

- Switch on the oven, then set it to 350 degrees F and let it preheat.
- Take a medium bowl, place the mashed banana in it and then stir in coconut until well combined.
- Take a large baking sheet, line it with a parchment sheet, and then scoop the prepared mixture on it, 2 tablespoons of mixture per cookie.
- Place the baking sheet into the refrigerator and then let it cool for 30 minutes or more until harden.

- Serve straight away.

Nutritional Information per Serving:

Calories: 51 Cal; Fat: 3 g; Protein: 0.2 g; Carbs: 4 g; Fiber: 1 g;

Chocolate Pots

Prep Time: 4 hours and 10 minutes; Cooking Time: 3 minutes; Yields: 4;

Ingredients:

- 6 ounces chocolate, unsweetened
- 1 cup Medjool dates, pitted
- 1 ¾ cups almond milk, unsweetened

Directions:

- Cut the chocolate into small pieces, place them in a heatproof bowl and then microwave for 2 to 3 minutes until melt completely, stirring every minute.
- Place dates in a blender, pour in the milk, and then pulse until smooth.
- Add chocolate into the blender and then pulse until combined.
- Divide the mixture into the small mason jars and then let them rest for 4 hours until set.
- Serve straight away.

Nutritional Information per Serving:

Calories: 321 Cal; Fat: 19 g; Protein: 6 g; Carbs: 34 g; Fiber: 4 g;

Maple and Tahini Fudge

Prep Time: 1 hour and 100 minutes; Cooking Time: 3 minutes; Yields: 15;

Ingredients:

- 1 cup dark chocolate chips, vegan
- ¼ cup maple syrup
- ½ cup tahini

Directions:

- Take a heatproof bowl, place chocolate chips in it and then microwave for 2 to 3 minutes until melt completely, stirring every minute.
- When melted, remove the chocolate bowl from the oven and then whisk in maple syrup and tahini until smooth.
- Take a 4-by-8 inches baking dish, line it with wax paper, spoon the chocolate mixture in it and then press it into the baking dish.
- Cover with another sheet with wax paper, press it down until smooth, and then let the fudge rest for 1 hour in the freezer until set.
- Then cut the fudge into 15 squares and serve.

Nutritional Information per Serving:

Calories: 110.7 Cal; Fat: 5.3 g; Protein: 2.2 g; Carbs: 15.1 g; Fiber: 1.6 g;

Creamsicles

Prep Time: 4 hours and 5 minutes; Cooking Time: 0 minutes; Yields: 5;

Ingredients:

- 3 tablespoons agave syrup
- 1 cup coconut milk, unsweetened
- ½ teaspoon vanilla extract, unsweetened
- 1 cup of orange juice

Directions:

- Place all the ingredients in a food processor or blender and then pulse until combined.
- Pour the mixture into five molds of Popsicle pan, insert a stick into each mold and then let it freeze for a minimum of 4 hours until hard.
- Serve when ready.

Nutritional Information per Serving:

Calories: 152 Cal; Fat: 10 g; Protein: 1 g; Carbs: 16 g; Fiber: 1 g;

Peanut Butter, Nut, and Fruit Cookies

Prep Time: 30 minutes; Cooking Time: 0 minutes; Yields: 25 cookies;

Ingredients:

- ¾ cup rolled oats
- ½ cup coconut flakes, unsweetened
- ¼ cup and 2 tablespoons chopped cranberries, dried
- ¼ cup sliced almonds
- ¼ cup and 2 tablespoons raisins
- ¼ cup maple syrup
- ¾ cup peanut butter

Directions:

- Take a baking sheet, line it with wax paper, and then set it aside until required.
- Take a large bowl, place oats, almonds, and coconut flakes in it, add ¼ cup each of cranberries and raisins, and then stir until combined.
- Add maple syrup and peanut butter, stir until well combined, and then scoop the mixture on the prepared baking sheet with some distance between them.
- Flatten each scoop of cookie mixture slightly, press remaining cranberries and raisins into each cookie, and then let it chill for 20 minutes until firm.
- Serve straight away.

Nutritional Information per Serving:

Calories: 140 Cal; Fat: 7 g; Protein: 3 g; Carbs: 18 g; Fiber: 5 g;

Chocolate Covered Dates

Prep Time: 1 hour and 10 minutes; Cooking Time: 3 minutes; Yields: 16;

Ingredients:

- 16 Medjool dates, pitted
- ½ teaspoon of sea salt
- ¾ cup almonds
- 1 teaspoon coconut oil
- 8 ounces chocolate chips, vegan

Directions:

- Take a medium baking sheet, line it with parchment paper, and then set aside until required.
- Place an almond into the pit of each date and then wrap the date tightly around it.

- Place chocolate chips in a heatproof bowl, add oil, and then microwave for 2 to 3 minutes until chocolate melts, stirring every minute.
- Working on one date at a time, dip each date into the chocolate mixture and then place it onto the prepared baking sheet.
- Sprinkle salt over the prepared dates and then let them rest in the refrigerator for 1 hour until chocolate is firm.
- Serve straight away.

Nutritional Information per Serving:

Calories: 179 Cal; Fat: 7.7 g; Protein: 3 g; Carbs: 28.5 g; Fiber: 3 g;

Hot Chocolate

Prep Time: 5 minutes; Cooking Time: 10 minutes; Yields: 4;

Ingredients:

- ¼ cup of cocoa powder
- 1/8 teaspoon salt
- ½ teaspoon vanilla extract, unsweetened
- ¼ cup of coconut sugar
- 3 cups almond milk, unsweetened

Directions:

- Take a medium saucepan, add salt, sugar, and cocoa powder in it, whisk until combined, and then whisk in milk.
- Place the pan over medium-high heat and then bring the milk mixture to a simmer and turn hot, continue whisking.
- Divide the hot chocolate evenly into four mugs and then serve.

Nutritional Information per Serving:

Calories: 137 Cal; Fat: 3 g; Protein: 6 g; Carbs: 21 g; Fiber: 2 g;

Vanilla Cupcakes

Prep Time: 10 minutes; Cooking Time: 20 minutes; Yields: 18;

Ingredients:

- 2 cups white whole-wheat flour
- 1 cup of coconut sugar
- ½ teaspoon salt
- 2 teaspoons baking powder
- 1 ¼ teaspoons vanilla extract, unsweetened
- ½ teaspoon baking soda
- 1 tablespoon apple cider vinegar
- ½ cup coconut oil, melted
- 1 ½ cups almond milk, unsweetened

Directions:

- Switch on the oven, then set it to 350 degrees F, and then let it preheat.
- Meanwhile, take a medium bowl, place vinegar in it, stir in milk, and then let it stand for 5 minutes until curdled.
- Take a large bowl, place flour in it, add salt, baking soda and powder, and sugar and then stir until mixed.
- Take a separate large bowl, pour in curdled milk mixture, add vanilla and coconut oil and then whisk until combined.
- Whisk almond milk mixture into the flour mixture until smooth batter comes together, and then spoon the mixture into two 12-cups muffin pans lined with muffin cups.
- Bake the muffins for 15 to 20 minutes until firm and the top turn golden brown, and then let them cool on the wire rack completely.
- Serve straight away.

Nutritional Information per Serving:

Calories: 152.4 Cal; Fat: 6.4 g; Protein: 1.5 g; Carbs: 22.6 g; Fiber: 0.5 g;

Chocolate Mug Cake

Prep Time: 5 minutes; Cooking Time: 3 minutes; Yields: 1;

Ingredients:

- 4 tablespoons white whole-wheat flour
- 2 tablespoons cocoa powder, unsweetened
- 3 tablespoons coconut sugar
- ¼ teaspoon baking powder
- 3 tablespoons soy milk
- 1 tablespoon coconut flakes, toasted
- 4 tablespoons applesauce
- 1 tablespoon chocolate chips, vegan

Directions:

- Take a mug, place flour in it, add baking powder, cocoa powder, and sugar and then stir until mixed.
- Take a medium bowl, pour in the milk, and then stir in applesauce until combined.
- Pour the milk mixture into the mug, whisk until smooth batter comes together, fold in chocolate chips, and then sprinkle coconut flakes on top.
- Microwave the prepared batter for 3 minutes at high heat setting until set and then serve.

Nutritional Information per Serving:

Calories: 448.8 Cal; Fat: 12.8 g; Protein: 8.4 g; Carbs: 87.2 g; Fiber: 8.5 g;

CONCLUSION

And there you have it. If there is one thing to take away from this book, it is that consistency is key. All progress will be lost if you do not stick to the routine. You can go about this at your own pace, and that is totally fine. Any progress, no matter how small, is a big win. All of that will compound into significant changes a few weeks down the line.

Health is a long journey that you might need to do for the rest of your life. Ideally, you want to start as soon as possible to get those benefits as fast as possible. Whatever you do, do not give up. You will begin to see the improvement in your own health before long.

With all that said, good luck on your vegan journey.

ABOUT THE AUTHOR

Anne Merritt is a well-known nutrition and health expert with over twenty years' experience in the field.

Inspired to follow a healthier lifestyle, she decided to change her diet and go vegan. After discovering the many benefits of following a plant-based diet, she knew it was something she'd dedicate her life to spreading the word about.

Anne's goal is to share her knowledge and experience with other people. Hopefully, her books will help you improve your life.

Manufactured by Amazon.ca
Bolton, ON